# The Inner Wealth Initiative

## THE NURTURED HEART APPROACH™

### for Educators

# The Inner Wealth Initiative

## THE NURTURED HEART APPROACH™
## for Educators

by **Tom Grove**, M.A.

and **Howard Glasser**, M.A.

with **Melissa Lynn Block**, M.Ed.

# The Inner Wealth Initiative

## THE NURTURED HEART APPROACH™
### for Educators

For information contact: Nurtured Heart Publications
4165 West Ironwood Hill Drive
Tucson, Arizona 85745
Email: adhddoc@theriver.com

For information about bulk purchasing discounts of this book or other Transforming the Difficult Child books, videos, or DVDs, please contact Fulfillment Services at 800-311-3132. For orders within the book industry, contact Brigham Distributing at 435-723-6611.

Cover photograph by Alice Rose Glasser.
Book design by Richard Diffenderfer.
Copy editing by Chris Howell.
Printed by Vaughan Printing, Nashville, TN.

Library of Congress Card Catalog Number: Pending

ISBN 0-9670507-7-4

Printed in the United States

First Printing: January 2007

*This book is dedicated to Maria Figueroa
and her wonderful staff at Tolson Elementary
in Tucson—and all those other courageous
educators around the world who are pioneering
this path of light for future generations.*

*To all of you—
Thank you for shining the light of greatness
into the eyes of our children.*

# About the Authors

**Tom Grove**, M.A., L.M.F.T.

Tom Grove is a licensed Marriage and Family Therapist at the Mental Health Center of Champaign in Champaign, Illinois, who earned his Master of Arts in experimental psychology from Eastern Illinois University. He divides his time between his therapy practice and helping schools implement the Nurtured Heart Approach. He has given numerous presentations and consultations to mental health providers, parents, and educators. He is a regular contributor to the advanced Nurtured Heart Approach training held in Tucson.

**Howard Glasser**, M.A.

Howard Glasser is the founder of Children's Success Foundation and designer of the Nurtured Heart Approach. He and Jennifer Easley are the co-authors of *Transforming the Difficult Child: The Nurtured Heart Approach* (1999), currently the top selling book on the topic of ADHD. He is also the author of *101 Reasons to Avoid Ritalin Like the Plague* (2005). He has been a featured guest on CNN and a consultant on *48 Hours*.

He lectures in the U.S. and internationally, teaching therapists, educators, and parents about the Nurtured Heart Approach, which is now being used in hundreds of thousands of homes and classrooms around the world.

Howard is former director and clinical supervisor of the Center for the Difficult Child in Tucson. He has been a consultant for numerous psychiatric, judicial, and educational programs. Although he has done extensive doctoral work in the fields of Clinical Psychology and Educational Leadership, he feels his own years as a difficult child contributed the most to his understanding of the needs of challenging children and to the success of his approach. He lives in Tucson, Arizona.

## Melissa Lynn Block, M.Ed.

Melissa Lynn Block is a writer and editor who specializes in helping others put their brilliant ideas, methods, and stories down on the printed page in the most clear, elegant, and accessible form. Her company, *ideokinesis,* has clients from many disciplines, including physicians, therapists, and educators. She has written, ghostwritten, and co-authored more than a dozen books, along with many articles and newsletters and a lot of Web content. She lives with her husband, two children, two stepchildren (part-time), cat, and five chickens in Santa Barbara, California. She can be contacted at ideokinesis@verizon.net.

### A Note about Gender Usage

In this book, we have used male and female gender references in a way that we hope represents both genders equally. Instead of using confusing "his or her" sentence constructions that strenuously try to represent male and female in every instance, we used one or the other gender in a more or less random way.

As we put clarity ahead of political correctness in importance, we hope that no one will read any gender stereotypes into our choice of gender usage in any part of this book.

### A Note about the Word *Positivity*

Positivity is not an actual word (yet!). But in trying to convey the Nurtured Heart Approach to our readers, we attempted to use other (actual) words and found they either had some interpretive baggage or didn't adequately convey our desired meaning. And since negativity is a word, we felt that it's opposite—positivity—would convey the proper level of vastness we were seeking in our attempts to fully describe the counterpoint of negativity. We therefore took the liberty, in this book, of "inventing" the word positivity to connote the richest sense of being positive. Again, we hope that readers will overlook our incorrectness in this situation and understand our motives.

—*Tom, Howie, and Melissa*

# Acknowledgements

GOD HAS CERTAINLY BLESSED MY LIFE even in times when it first didn't seem so. I thank Him for it all. Whatever good I am able to do comes from Him. I am also deeply blessed by and thankful for my wife and children. It was love at first sight and still is. They are the joy of my life.

Howard Glasser is an indispensable part of my life. His wisdom and friendship are trustworthy companions. He is a brother to me, as well as a guide. He is very, very alive. Needless to say, I would still be searching for a powerful way to help people have hope and value in themselves and their lives if not for his amazing creation. It is from the deepest part of his heart that he designed the Nurtured Heart Approach. I thank him for his fearless belief in the hearts of everyone, for helping us all see beauty in tiny moments, and for giving us a pathway to triumph over the deepest doubt.

There are many others to thank in the journey that led to the creation of this book. The Mental Health Board of Champaign County was invaluable in promoting the vision for and funding of my work. The tenacious advocacy of Juli Kartel at the Mental Health Center of Champaign has been a great comfort and inspiration. If she had her way, the Nurtured Heart Approach would have been used even in the most remote villages of the world since at least 2002. I am deeply grateful to the City of Champaign Middle School principals who have supported this approach and welcomed me into their schools: Dr. Carol Stack, Joe Williams and particularly Dr. Susan Zola. Her wisdom and her spirit for her school abound. She is on a mission to bring forth the best of every student and every teacher at every moment.

None of this support and leadership would mean anything without the incredible bravery, dedication, and love of the teachers who have taken this training on. They have been the volunteers willing to test all the ideas in this book. Many times they have brought me to the brink of tears as they reached with their hearts directly into the hearts of students, transforming them forever. They change lives. They have changed mine.

The classroom nurturing of Natasha Harroff, the megawatt personality of Brian Yacko, and the respectful compassion of Linda Seaman have changed many a life. They have put the lost back on a path of light, healed wounded souls, and deepened the blessings of those already greatly blessed. Others who have so positively influenced not only their students but also me include Mr. Pickell, Ms. McFarlane,

Ms. Powell, Ms. Atkinson, Ms. Palmer, Ms. Prilliman, Mr. Craig, and Ms. Steinman. The mission work of Ms. Cowsert to bring inner wealth to the hearing impaired in her classes and in Jamaica is truly inspiring. The teachers and administrators at Jefferson Middle School have awed me with the strength and depth with which they have embraced this approach. Thank you for having me in your classrooms to witness your powerful zeal for the future generations to come.

I echo Howie's acknowledgements of the excellent and gracious work of Melissa and Chris to make this book an inspiring and practical guide. I give you both my thanks.

Lisa Bravo and Gabrielli LaChiara, you are so dear to me. Songs in my heart each of you. I sing them often.

—*Tom Grove*

THIS BOOK IS A COLLABORATION between a method that I've had the honor to "midwife" and a man who has made it his life's passion to optimize its use in education.

The method is the Nurtured Heart Approach, and I am eternally grateful for the grace, joy and fulfillment it brings to my life. The man is Tom Grove, who has taken his great skills as a therapist and wrapped them around powerful notions of how to help children feel and experience inner wealth. Tom has evolved the language and practice of the Nurtured Heart Approach, and for that I am also eternally grateful.

I am also eternally grateful to Melissa Lynn Block for her incredible collaborative and literary skills in bringing all the pieces of this puzzle together. She has been masterful in bringing order and direction to this project.

As always, I am so grateful to Chris Howell for the daunting task of bringing this text to a final and perfected form. We asked more than ever from her on this project and she, as always, was more than equal to the task. Her work is so great and so appreciated!

I am grateful to The Author's Team and Mahesh Grossman for helping bring us all together.

Many thanks to Richard Diffenderfer for his wonderful design talent in getting the manuscript ready for print, a hugely underrated part of the process.

I am also so grateful to my wonderful daughter Alice Glasser for once again lending her artistic talent to the making of the front cover. Her love and support are so great and so appreciated.

I give unending thanks to Maria Figueroa, the incredible principal at Tolson Elementary in Tucson, Arizona, for being a forerunner in this great experiment of impacting the lives of our youth and showing the immense power of inner wealth. She will forever be my hero; she deftly demonstrates that a principal can make things happen in a hurry.

Great thanks also to all those others who are at the cutting edge of bringing the Nurtured Heart Approach to education, proving there are so many hearts so ready to be nurtured and so many levels of rippling success to be gained when this nurturing happens. To all those advanced trainers who are making this endeavor a large part of their lives and missions, I am also so grateful.

Finally, I am eternally grateful to Grace and Spirit for designating me for this role and this journey. The support of the universe is endless, ever-present and utterly inspiring.

—*Howie Glasser*

I WOULD FIRST AND FOREMOST LIKE TO THANK Howard Glasser for giving me the opportunity to write about his approach. As a writer and as a parent, it's an enormous pleasure for me to work on a project that has such potential for creating and propagating positive change in children's lives. Collaborating with Howie is—as one might expect when learning about his work—a joyful, positive process.

Thanks to Tom Grove for moving through this process with trust, courage, generosity, and commitment. He's so full of energy and drive to help others succeed that one can't help but catch the bug, and his writings fairly burst with enthusiasm! Tom's grounded understanding of the application of the Nurtured Heart Approach, gained in real time in real classrooms working with real teachers and students, was an invaluable part of the project for all of us.

Thanks to Mahesh Grossman for bringing us all together, and to my children for being the reason I do what I do. Thanks to my mom and dad and siblings for being such great friends and supporters. And thanks as always to my most valued critic and perfect counterpart, my husband Patrick.

—*Melissa Lynn Block*

# Contents

# Foreword

*This comes straight from the heart of Dawn Duncan-Lewis, Therapist/School Counselor at Skagit Discovery Center in Sedro-Woolley, Washington*

SKAGIT DISCOVERY CENTER is a school for kids with special needs. Most have behavioral challenges and some have mental health impairment. Our 25 to 35 students are K-12 and come from 14 different school districts in four counties. They are the most challenging children in their school districts. Our school is, for some, the last stop before hospitalization or group care.

Our faculty includes a principal, a counselor, a half-time case manager, an administrative assistant, four lead teachers, and eight instructional assistants. The school is operated by the Northwest Educational Service District 189, a co-op whose mission is to support the school districts in our area. I am under contract to the school, employed by Catholic Social Services.

When I first came to Skagit Discovery Center at the beginning of the 2003-2004 school year, I was struck by the level of energy I observed in the halls. The children's hugely intense feelings showed in their bodies, voices and language. I noticed that, when I used my counselor skills and listened to them, replying softly, they seemed to calm fairly quickly, especially if they were in my office and we were alone. But the "fix" was usually short-lived.

One day, I noticed a 13-year-old boy lying on the floor in the alcove near his classroom door. He was waving his arm at me and cursing, yet imploring me to spend time with him. I realized that I was beginning to feel claustrophobic. Scenes from two movies came to mind: one was *Bedlam* from the 1940s, the scene where a woman was entering a poor house/mental institution and people were wailing and waving their arms at her; the second, the scene from the 1960s original *Night of the Living Dead* where zombies are approaching a living person in a graveyard. You do not know exactly what it is they want of the person, but you have a feeling that, if they catch up with him, he will be overwhelmed and ultimately creamed.

At the same time these seemingly out-of-control students were in the hall, many of our students were busy, in their classrooms, doing their work and benefiting from the relationships and instruction provided there. I have no doubt that as a staff, we were doing the very best we could to help the students who were so bent on finding their way out of the classroom. But despite our best efforts to guide and motivate them, I remember thinking, "Has it always been this way? There must be a greater wisdom out there."

In May 2004, the end of my first school year at Discovery, my supervisor at Catholic Community Services asked me to attend a training where I would learn about something called the Nurtured Heart Approach. It was an all-day training in Seattle and I thought, "How can I be gone a whole day?" But I went. I remember standing in the lobby during intermission talking to my colleagues. We were all trying to process something that felt of an earth-shaking nature. I had a feeling that life as I knew it would be different after that day.

When I presented the idea of adopting the Nurtured Heart Approach to Skagit's principal, Ken Chovil, he liked the idea and agreed that we should begin to implement the approach right away. Needless to say, I was very excited. Ken and I started training the staff in the Nurtured Heart Approach as soon as school was out that year, and we picked it up again when the new school year started.

Our somewhat clumsy and uncertain first attempts to apply the approach with our kids did not go unnoticed by them. When we recognized their successes out loud, the younger kids' whole bodies moved toward us like a time-lapse photo of a sunflower moving toward the sun! From the high school students, we heard comments like "What are you doing? Quit being so nice!" But the rooms got quieter and teachers just kept on handing out bonus points.

Within a few weeks, the principal and I noticed a huge difference. THERE WAS NO ONE IN THE HALL! DAY AFTER DAY! NO ONE! Ken and I went through a bit of an identity crisis. We didn't feel needed by the staff to put out crisis fires anymore. The kids were not seeking us out for that "attention-drink-of-water" they had so fervently sought from us before. I walked around not knowing what to do. Then it occurred to me: I needed to figure out my new role as support person to all of these "natural therapists." The kids were now getting their needs met by their teachers in the classroom!

During that second year, I was attending classes at City University to get certified as a school counselor to add to my therapist credentials. Toward the end of the year, I needed some data to complete a paper on "The Process of Change." I wondered what would happen if I could compare data for students who were at our school both the first year I was there and the second when we used the Nurtured Heart Approach. I decided to use Incident Report data, which involved our most challenging students.

Ken asked me to see whether my data could reflect the intensity of the incidents, so I decided to break up the Incident Reports into types of events, such as damage to property, physical aggression toward others, or running from school. I found myself holding, for one student, a stack of reports in one hand for the first year that was one and one-half inches thick, and in my other hand for the second year, I had a stack only a quarter-inch thick. I told the principal, "Now that's a visual!" The results of this study on our seven most challenging students: the Incident Reports contained 518 total items for the school year 2003/2004, while only 94 items were listed for the year 2004/2005 (data did not include the last 21 days of that school year). That amounted to an 82 percent improvement!

Another way that we noticed change in our students was revealed through the use of a developmental assessment we discovered at about the same time we learned about the Nurtured Heart Approach. This assessment is part of a program called Developmental Therapy/Developmental Teaching [Wood, M.M., Davis, K.R., Swindle, F.H. & Quirk, C.A. (1996). Developmental therapy-developmental teaching (3rd ed.). Austin, TX: ProEd.]. The students who come to us are chronologically 5 to18 years of age, but the assessments almost always show that they are much younger than their age in areas of behavior and socialization; this would be one way of explaining the impulsivity, poor problem-solving skills, and tendency to display tantrum-type behavior. When we performed the assessment a second time a few months after implementing the Nurtured Heart Approach, we found that *all of them* had matured developmentally. Many had matured one whole stage, and a few two stages, within a few months!

I have many remarkable stories I could tell, but I can sum up the differences I observed in our students by saying that, before we used the Nurtured Heart Approach, our "kids in the hall" were not able to interact effectively with their environment. Some seemed pre-verbal and could barely talk. After the intervention, they were sitting across from me like young versions of grown-ups, telling me about their lives, thoughts, frustrations and even goals for their future! With the students' permission – and they rarely refused – I could use that information to more fully introduce these students to their teachers. I was reminded of the movie *Awakenings* – and this was before I knew that the real-life *Awakenings* doctor did the intro for Howie Glasser's website! We literally watched these students "wake up!"

The Nurtured Heart Approach makes the world a better place for everyone. We had a teacher comment early on, "I actually enjoy coming to work now!" Another teacher said: "Nurtured Heart is invigorating. It makes you say, 'Oh gosh, *yes!*'"

The Nurtured Heart Approach is very powerful for working with parents and fellow staff members as well. It provides us a way to *nourish* each other with nutrients we all are craving. It's a guilt-free win-win program that doesn't involve pointing fingers at anyone. The Nurtured Heart Approach makes it easier for us all to be our best as we help our children.

—*Dawn Duncan-Lewis, M.S., L.M.F.T.*

# Preface

## The Birth of the Nurtured Heart Approach

### by HOWARD GLASSER

MY LIFE'S WORK has been to create a non-drug approach for working with intense or difficult children. In the years since I created this approach, it has proven itself with tens of thousands of children. The approach I developed—or, rather, that developed me—is called the Nurtured Heart Approach.

When I first began working with families that had difficult children, it seemed as though every intervention that *should* have helped did not. What's more, it became evident to me that my suggestions—born out of my clinical psychology training and the skills I acquired while studying with some interesting people and reading some fascinating books—all seemed to actually make the situation *worse*.

Frustrated with my ineffectiveness at helping these families, I was tempted to throw in the towel and go back to working with adults and therapeutic milieus—fields where I had experienced a good deal of success in prior years. But some epiphanies in me ultimately inspired me to stick with it. These epiphanies changed my life dramatically and led to the birth of my approach.

♥

I BEGAN TO HAVE A MEMORY OF MY OWN LIFE as an exquisitely difficult child. In my bones, I could feel all the memories and sensations that I had tried to forget, especially in relation to family dynamics. This coincided with a period of time where I couldn't quiet down even for a minute without my internal message service sounding the bell that I had "mail" (i.e., more sensations, recollections and strange ideas). Call it what you want: intuition, channeling, transmissions from another planet. Wherever they came from, these ideas seemed…well, *silly*. I couldn't seem to rid myself of these ridiculous notions that were flooding my life.

In the beginning, I dismissed whatever came through as irrelevant. At some point, though, I started to bring pieces into my work with difficult children and their families. I was consistently floored by the immediate positive response I saw in the adults and their children. Those silly ideas that had pestered me interminably appeared to grab the parents I worked with in a novel way. I could see them saying to themselves, "Oh, YES, that makes total sense!" Time and again, these ideas created experiences so powerful that my clients couldn't seem to wait to put them into motion and affect changes in the lives of their children.

Here's one of those silly ideas that kept hounding me and that proved to be enormously useful to parents of difficult children: I started to see adults as children's favorite toys. I would encourage parents I worked with to think about how a child responds when he receives a new toy. He's likely to spend time exploring all it has to offer, adventurously experiencing all the toy's responses to his manipulations. The typical toy has features, and whether there are ten, a hundred, or a hundred thousand, some will be exciting and engaging, while others might be boring.

I encouraged parents to imagine how children tend to go back to a boring feature to see if it might change, but once they determine that it is truly and predictably boring, they write it off and refuse to interact with that aspect of the toy.

Once parents grasped this concept, I would ask them, "How many features do *we* have?" Adults have virtually unlimited nuances of movement, expression, mood, and emotion. And there are practically limitless ways we can respond, connect, and demonstrate closeness and animation. An adult is, for all intents and purposes, *the ultimate toy.*

This would lead to a discussion of how kids are continually in the process of drinking in the world. They are forming impressions about how the world around them works and their impact upon it from the day they are born. My strong intuitive belief—which has been borne out with the success of the approach founded on this belief—is that children who are more needy, intense, and/or sensitive than the next child, when exposed to traditional or conventional styles of parenting and teaching, form impressions in a specific way that leads to challenging behavior issues later on. This is because they see that the adults in their lives, their ultimate toys, are much more interesting when things are going *wrong* than when things are going right. We adults have far more captivating, energized, animated responses to children when there is adversity.

Adults tend to be more tuned-in when things are going wrong, displaying more emotion, discussion, relationship, intimacy, and presence. When things are going well—when the child isn't having issues or problems—we, the toys, are relatively boring. We tend to have relatively little presence, not much to say, and don't give much energy to what we do say. Just as is the case with real toys, the child is more likely to write us off and to attach herself with even greater determination to the ways and means of tapping into the mother lode: *greater levels of presence.* Children need adult presence and energy, and the more they can get out of us, the better. Usually, the most reliable way to get this out of their favorite toys in a hurry is by creating conflict, chaos, and disruption.

An intense or difficult child is more likely to require adult presence and energy in greater doses and frequency. The average child might see the negative responses of an adult toward adversity as enough of a deterrent to stop pushing those buttons—although that child might still crave more intense presence and energy from the adult. *But with the typical "difficult" child, the need for the figurative bells, whistles, and flashing lights that spring forth on their favorite toys when things go wrong is greater than their need for approval.* They are not doing this on purpose; rather, they are drawn, almost magnetically, to the greater, more intriguing level of response.

If adults can energize their approval, recognition, and praise *when things are going right*, the features of the adult "toy" suddenly become much more engaging when the child is doing the right things. When we also make a concerted effort to downplay the energy and focus a child gets in response to negative behavior, we take all the excitement out of those features of the toy that once were so fascinating.

This "adults as children's favorite toys" notion, along with many other related ideas that had hounded my thoughts, were placed into my therapeutic bag of tricks and became the basis of what I had to offer to my clients. In Tucson, where I live and work, no one else seemed to be getting results with these children, so when I did, people wanted to know what I was doing. I initially refused to tell them for two reasons: first, because I thought that this approach was too idiosyncratic and silly; and second, because I hated public speaking and felt there was no way to even begin to coherently explain to other professionals what I was doing.

I was terrified that the concepts and practices I was developing, and with which I was getting greater and greater results, would get me laughed out of the therapeutic community. As it all continued to "cook" together and become a cohesive approach, word got out, and I got more challenging cases. And these challenging cases helped me a great deal to bring the approach to more powerful levels.

Eventually, my arm was twisted by an agency to which I was indebted. I agreed to do an in-service—and hated it, promising myself I would never do it again. But then, two months later, I was grocery shopping when a man introduced himself as someone who had heard my talk. He turned out to be the head of the family preservation unit at the agency where I spoke—that's code for the department that deals with consistently challenging children and situations—and supervised 10 counselors there. Most of his counselors, he told me, were already using this approach exclusively, with great results. Apparently, there was no turning back.

♥

AS A THERAPIST who has spent years working with difficult children who fall easily into the category of ADHD, I have come to believe that whenever we hand this diagnosis to a child, we are dealing not with an incurable neurobiological disorder, but with a programming problem. The adults in his life are, more than likely, trying as hard as they can to help this child with one of (roughly) thousands of conventional approaches—none of which in my belief has a chance of facilitating transformation in a child who is not wired like the average child.

I would never argue that there is a shortage of children who meet the legislated criteria for ADHD. There are plenty of children who are impulsive, distractible, annoying, difficult, and challenging—in all the ways that are specifically profiled in the Diagnostic and Statistical Manual of Mental Disorders. To me, the bigger issue is to find out whether these very same children, exposed to a different kind of programming—a style or approach applied by one or more influential adults in their lives—can avoid the pitfalls of the ADHD diagnosis.

Can these children channel the intensity that has caused them such difficulty in the past into a positive quality that propels them to achieve greatness? Most definitely, yes. Instead of calling it a disorder and suppressing it with drugs, can we call it intensity and find a way to bring it forth constructively and beautifully? Yes, and it really works. Case in point: Tolson Elementary School in Tucson, Arizona. In a nutshell, Tolson's results over the past seven years have been awe-inspiring.

Only one child has been suspended (twice), not one child has been referred for ADHD evaluation, and not a single child has been referred for medications! Expenditures on special education services have dropped dramatically in this school—from the previous 15% of all students to a current level of under 2%. Teacher attrition, which had been over 50 percent annually, has now been at *zero* for the past three years. Scores on standardized tests have risen dramatically. The school's principal, who has received regional recognition for the positive test score change, is fond of saying that although the faculty prizes and encourages academic accomplishment, they do not teach to the test.

Certainly the school still gets at least its fair share of children at risk, those in low socioeconomic brackets and minorities who are traditionally at greater risk of underachievement and behavior problems. But the school is now wired to propel these children toward their destinies of greatness. I have been so inspired by the transformations that I formed the Children's Success Foundation, which has the mission of bringing the Nurtured Heart Approach to educational communities. An entire school district in Connecticut is moving into its first year using the approach.

My belief is that, in addition to improved test scores and dramatic decreases in medication use, ADHD diagnosis, teacher attrition, and special education services, broader use of this approach in schools will significantly reduce drop-out rates, cigarette, alcohol, and drug use, and teen pregnancy. I predict that we will see higher rates of college entrance. Districts will save enormous financial resources: a decline from 15 percent utilization of special education services to 10 percent in a district of 10,000 children would save three million dollars each year. Then, we can truly have a version of "No Child Left Behind" that serves our nation's educational vision.

♥

The reason that this approach works so well is that it cultivates something I call *inner wealth*—the ability to feel successful, cope, be happy, and grow within ourselves and with other people. Inner wealth is a multifaceted inner experience of our greatness and deeply connected to our feeling that we have meaning—that we are important just by virtue of being alive.

Tolson principal Maria Figueroa's experience—and my own—bears out that children who come to experience inner wealth do not need to be coerced into preparing for and doing well on tests; rather, they *desire* to do well. They want to show up ready to participate. They want to do their homework and schoolwork and perform well, no matter what their home situation might be. Teachers call home to report progress and success instead of problems.

All this is accomplished simply by the adults choosing to be attentive to the children's choices to *not* break the rules and to make other good decisions that promote cooperation, care, learning, and positive relationship. Instead of adults firing off tired, under-energized, vague statements like "good job" and "thank you," they are making more elaborate statements of appreciation and recognition from the heart—external statements that lead a child to experience a first-hand internal experience of success. Not just any successes, but successes that resonate at deeper-than-ordinary levels of the human condition.

We can go well beyond improvements to transformation, where children find their greatness while they are still young. They won't have to go on a mad search for it in their adult years, like so many of us had to do.

Our transformed, flourishing youth won't have a legacy of believing that the best way to achieve presence with self or others is through negativity. Rather, they will stand a great chance of truly enjoying people and life itself in a straightforward, congruent way. It's an entirely different dance than the ones we often see in our educational institutions, and it's a lovely dance.

*Blessings & Miracles,*
*Howard Glasser, M.A.*

# Introduction

## *Why the Nurtured Heart Approach Belongs in Schools*

SCHOOLS MAY WELL BE OUR MOST VIABLE HOPE FOR A BETTER SOCIETY. Five days a week, nine or more months a year, students are a captive audience, learning everything from reading and history to impressions about whom and what they are and who they are likely to become. They are being taught how valuable they are, how much they belong in the stream of life, and how likely they are to have friends, a good and happy life, or an impact on the community.

Teachers, administrators, office staff, janitors, aides, volunteers and other students constantly send each other messages about these lessons. Every time we smile at one another, every time we avoid a glance, every time we speak, and every time we look up to see what another person is doing, we send a message. We cannot avoid doing this. Even in trying *not* to send a message, we send one. Children are on the lookout for those messages all the time as they try to figure out who and what they will be in this life.

As teachers and parents charged with sending those messages, the Nurtured Heart Approach gives us tools to consciously and caringly send the ones that are best—most encouraging, positive, and constructive—for the children and for the world they will eventually have to negotiate as adults.

Few people are as important to a young person as a teacher. No social environment outside the home is more encompassing and important than school. Children with a wonderful home life may be devastated by school; or the reverse may be true: school can elevate children above all obstacles.

As a teacher, you well know that you have an awesome and wonderful responsibility that goes far beyond the math or English or social studies knowledge you impart to your students. The Nurtured Heart Approach gives you a formula, a method, for sending positive and uplifting messages to every student, with focused intensity, no matter what subject or grade level you teach. And you'll find that those messages will transfer to other aspects of your life, and will lift *you*—as well as your students—into a more positive place.

Even while you read this, entire schools and teachers within schools are using this approach. Perhaps even an entire school district or several districts are implementing the Nurtured Heart Approach as you read these words.

♥

TEACHERS ARE BESET by many internal and external forces beyond their control. Curricula, budgets, administrations, policies, unions, parents, school boards and the building's facilities are but some of the factors pressing daily on many educators. Just getting some photocopies made is often a major challenge. The Nurtured Heart Approach is a tremendously helpful way to build teachers' faith and trust in themselves as professionals regardless of these fluctuating influences.

Administrators often don't have the tools to support teachers who are putting their hearts, souls, and sweat into their work. Co-author Tom Grove cites the following example. The most respected veteran teacher at one school lamented to Tom that the principal had not once set foot in her room during the school year's seven months. He had never told her how well her classes were going nor even struck up a conversation with her in passing. But the principal had told Tom several times that "Mrs. S" was an excellent teacher. Had he said this to "Mrs. S" as well, it might have made a tremendous difference. A school where the Nurtured Heart Approach is in place would be a school where the principal could do for teachers what teachers do for students: increase their inner wealth, which in turn helps them do their work with greater enthusiasm and confidence.

♥

IT ALL BEGAN at a school in Tucson, Arizona. Tolson Elementary School principal Maria Figueroa realized it was not the *academic* curriculum, but the *social* curriculum (the messages being "taught" about the value of each person and about how people optimally relate to one another) that was driving suspensions, teacher burnout, classroom problems, academic failure, mental heath referrals, and medication referrals in her school. She realized that the Nurtured Heart Approach was a way to deliver a social curriculum with messages of value, competence, and belonging. She has made her vision a reality for thousands of students.

Tolson Elementary is a school of over 500 students, 81 percent of whom qualify for free and reduced lunch programs, meaning that they typically are disadvantaged children facing poverty, family stresses, and limited access to health care resources. At eight times the district average, Tolson used to have the highest rate of suspensions among the more than 60 schools in the district.

In 1999, the principal implemented Howard Glasser's Nurtured Heart Approach school-wide. Since the Nurtured Heart Approach became integrated into the school's classrooms, Tolson has had only one student suspended; no referrals to the juvenile justice system; no bullying; dramatic decreases in referrals for special education; no referrals for ADHD evaluations; and no new children on ADHD medications. Teacher attrition also fell dramatically. And Tolson's standardized test scores have risen dramatically.

These amazing and sustained improvements are not the result of a better or different academic curriculum, but of a dramatically improved social curriculum. It is a curriculum of *inner wealth*. It is a curriculum where school personnel can convincingly "teach" students that, just by virtue of their existence, they are *already* amazing, likeable, wonderful people. Tolson's example clearly demonstrates that children who are "convinced" of their greatness will manifest it as a reality.

And as you learn to see and point out the best in your students, you will learn to do the same for yourself and for everyone, adult or child, with whom you interact. Even if you're already a joyful person who feels successful in work and at home, this book will raise your expectations and build on the joy you already have.

♥

THE TOLSON STATISTICS are compelling. Huge amounts of money can be saved when teacher turnover is low, attendance is up, less staff and less time are spent on behavior problems, the use of substitutes declines, and people help rather than fight each other.

Using rich relationships balanced with clear limits, the Nurtured Heart Approach increases time actually spent teaching, student achievement, and grades. Children are less worried, less stressed, and less distracted. Special education costs plummet.

Everyone in the school can see the impact of using this approach day after day. Being liked and loved, for 30-plus hours a week, is great therapy. Teachers and other school staff will feel effective at helping students overcome problems—or at least make school a place where students can thrive despite problems elsewhere. Students will truly sense that they are living in a sea of positivity while at school.

How many gifted students have you met who perform poorly due to lack of effort? How many low-average students have you seen pour their hearts into something and succeed tremendously? That willingness to make a big effort is founded in relationships with important adults, including parents and teachers. Once the child's internal sense of greatness takes hold deep within, he can take that sense of well-being with him through every relationship, joy, sorrow, and challenge he faces in his lifetime.

The Nurtured Heart Approach is an architecture and a process that's about creating relationships that energize and support success and positive choices. It has many applications, but this book is about its application in schools. The Nurtured Heart Approach is a curriculum of forgiveness and restoration: problems no longer define who you are or what you will become. It is also a curriculum of optimism and trust. Through it, school personnel demonstrate the highest expectations of students—teaching each student that there is *nothing* the student can do to lower those expectations or to prevent the staff from creating success as the only option.

The students no longer have to worry about being liked, strive for attention, or fear their problems. Teachers no longer have to fear their students, spend valuable time on discipline problems, or worry about being respected. In the best situations—where this curriculum is implemented school-wide, classroom by classroom—the entire school comes to inspiring levels of respect, emotional safety, and development of character. The natural outcome becomes greater academic achievement. At that point, as a teacher, you will see an amazing increase in your productivity in terms of how much actual teaching you are able to do!

# Chapter One

## Introduction to the Nurtured Heart Approach

*The teacher's job is as much a matter of creating the capacity to learn as it is a process of filling a predetermined capacity.*
—John Lounsbury, former head of the National Middle School Association, in *As I See It*, National Middle School Press, 1991.

CO-AUTHOR TOM GROVE, a therapist who guides the classroom application of the Nurtured Heart Approach, didn't recognize how much teachers needed this approach until the day he met separately with two teachers and asked each one "What is teaching like for you?" Both responded with tears. They felt isolated, helpless, and bad about themselves professionally.

Many new teachers have almost no preparation for the emotional and behavioral problems they will face on the job. The number of teachers who leave the profession within the first three years is around 30 percent, and only 50 percent make it past five years before they've had enough. Every school day in the United States on average, nearly 1,000 teachers leave the field of teaching, and another 1,000 change schools in search of a better situation.[1, 2, 3]

Surveys indicate that teachers leave the profession or switch schools because of inadequate administrative support, low salaries, and limited faculty input to the school's decision-making processes. Another major reason teachers quit: student discipline problems. Teacher education programs at universities rarely give new teachers adequate training for the kinds of children and issues they will find in their classrooms.

The difficulty schools have keeping teachers amounts to a full-blown crisis, costing American schools $2.6 billion every year. The cost to students who are forfeiting inspired, energetic, caring teachers cannot be measured. Attrition is worst in poorer schools and in schools with excessive discipline problems—arguably, the

---

1. www.all4ed.org/publications/TeacherAttrition.pdf, at the site of the Alliance for Excellent Education
2. Ingersoll, Richard M. and Thomas M. Smith, "The wrong solution to the teacher shortage," *Educational Leadership* 2003 May;60(8):30-33.
3. http://www.all4ed.org/publications/TappingThePotential/TappingThePotential.pdf

schools that most desperately need qualified and passionate teachers.

When the Nurtured Heart Approach enters a school, the positivity and focus on creating success affect everyone—teachers, administrators, and students. Sometimes, the parents of children at the school are so impressed by the changes they see in their children that they, too, are drawn to learn more about the approach.

## First, Create the Right Relationships

While schools are pressured to produce higher and higher levels of achievement, many have put the cart before the horse. The value of the student has been superseded by the value of the test score. Yes—test scores are important, and current trends reflect that we are losing ground to other nations academically. We believe that this has less to do with academic curricula and students' innate abilities and more to do with *the relationships that create the desire and capacity to learn.* In our opinion, these relationships are the foundation of academic achievement.

Teachers have repeatedly told Tom Grove and Howie Glasser that nothing prepared them for the types of students or the pace they would face. Of the 15 or so first-year teachers Tom met at one school, not one had received training to prepare them for difficult classrooms; and in an informal survey of several thousand teachers who attended his lectures and workshops, Howie found that fewer than one-half of one percent felt that they'd been adequately prepared in their university programs for what they ended up facing in classrooms. At a time when future educators would have been most receptive to approaches that worked, most were simply taught variations of conventional or traditional methods that don't stand a chance of working with a large number of children.

In a place of employment where you fit in and feel appreciated, you are more likely to stay—perhaps despite a less-than-optimum salary. You are seeking relationships that allow you to shine; that lend comfort and support; that help you move toward your inner potential for greatness. School administrators need their sense of success and inner wealth bolstered as well as teachers do. Districts are under tremendous pressure to legislate excellence via endless requirements and standards that often interfere not only with productivity, but also with schools' ability to provide a nurturing environment.

While excellence is obviously the desired objective, how is it produced? We believe that it boils down to having the right skills to empower and cultivate excellence in others. The Nurtured Heart Approach gives administrators and boards a powerful way to realize their dreams of an educational system benefiting all.

## A Social Curriculum That Meets
## the Challenges of Today's Classrooms

We are all made from the same matter and chemicals. It is our relationships that make all the difference. A person's relationship with herself affects every aspect of her existence. Change any pivotal aspect of how we view ourselves—of whom we have become through endeavors of relationship—and we well could be a vastly different person. *The Nurtured Heart Approach is a powerful and effective way to create great relationships.* It is especially well-suited for improving relationships in the contexts of families and schools.

You may think that there is no way to reach students and help them achieve; you may feel totally overwhelmed by the obstacles many students face in their daily lives and bring with them to the classroom. After all, many students have terrible home lives, live in or on the edge of poverty, or seem to have no interest in learning anything. Some are very withdrawn or sad. There are students with rich, wonderful home lives who have a bleak and unfulfilling school life. Others seem committed to finding new ways to torment adults and peers and show respect for no one—not even themselves.

There is no shortage of students who have dismal relationships with themselves, with others, and with life in general. The quest to feel worthy and competent, to belong, and to be happy extends to us all. Many teachers and parents wonder how they can find fulfillment in their work and at home. Until they do this for themselves, it's tough to guide the child—your student—to fulfillment in these areas.

This book is for you and those students. We hope to show you how to cultivate great relationships; from there, you'll see your classroom transform into one full of amazingly mature, achieving students.

This approach works because it creates an environment where students can't help but discover that they are successful and wonderful. They learn that they are already important and greatly valued by others, and they grow to accept this deep inside themselves. They realize that their problems are nothing compared to their ability to overcome them. This social curriculum, which becomes an integral part of the student that can be taken with him wherever he goes, cultivates a quality we call *inner wealth*.

## A Brief History of the Nurtured Heart Approach

The Nurtured Heart Approach was developed by Howard Glasser in the mid-1990s to address some of the severe behavior problems he encountered working with children. Traditional therapy approaches were ineffective in so many cases: many children seemed almost immune to such interventions, or any improvements were short-lived.

As he developed the basic foundation of the Nurtured Heart Approach, he began to see fast and deep change in children and the adults involved with them. Children who had seemed unreachable were connecting, thriving, and more joyful. Adults who seemed resentful, mean, burned-out, or helpless in dealing with these children became confident, renewed and happy to be beneficial for their child again.

Through the efforts of many people, this approach has expanded into schools, juvenile justice centers, HeadStart centers, treatment programs, teen pregnancy programs, therapy offices, and happier homes around the world.

## Nurtured Heart Approach In A Nutshell

Applied to the realm of education, this approach is directly aimed at creating thriving social environments in classrooms and in the entire school as well. This is accomplished by changing, if not reversing, some of the more "traditional" methods of classroom management.

It is not founded merely on accentuating the positive, as when we "catch the student being good," nor does it "take more traditional concepts a few notches further"—both common misconceptions in people who are in the early stages of learning about the approach. **It is an approach that completely reverses the traditional payoffs for students who act up by "creating"—if not "hijacking" them into—undeniable moments of success. It is an approach that renders problems unnecessary as a way of gaining and maintaining relationship. It transports students into an entirely different sense of who they are.**

The Nurtured Heart Approach is a long way from the common dictum that "the best discipline plan is a good lesson plan." We have frequently seen brilliant lessons eaten alive by discipline problems. We believe that the best discipline plan is a great *relationship* plan. By using this approach, you will enjoy wonderful relationships as a result of your social curriculum; and from that accomplishment, you will be able to realize your academic curriculum.

The foundations of the Nurtured Heart Approach can be broken down into a few basic principles:

1. **Your energy and relationship are the most valuable prizes you have to give anyone.** Each time you engage with, focus on, and interact with a student, you are giving him what he most needs from you. You can make use of both energy and relationship to deliberately speak, act, and interact with students in ways that encourage success.

2. **As the teacher, your energy is the most valuable prize in the classroom.** Students are constantly seeking relationship with you. This may seem hard to believe right now, but we assure you it is true. You are the most mature, wise, and knowledgeable messenger of the social curriculum in the room. Your opinions of and the messages you send to students carry tremendous value.

3. **Responding to students' problems with big doses of your energy is like throwing gasoline on a fire.** This teaches students that you have loads of relationship for them—*when problems come up.*

4. The object is to be *totally captured by success rather than by problems* and to learn how to effectively communicate this to your students. More than likely, if you were trained in traditional approaches to working with students, you respond with less energy when students are successful than when they are problematic. Our language of success is under-energized, as evidenced by our normal ways of praising. A "thank you" or "good job" is skimpy compared to the highly explicative language of failure most of us find effortless. We tend to demonstrate much more evidence of energy and relationship when things are going wrong instead of producing that energy and relationship in response to successes.

5. **Rules must be clear and their enforcement strict.** By strict, we don't mean severe. Strictness is about showing with absolute clarity where the line is drawn. There must be no ambivalence about the rules or what happens when they are broken. The clearer and stricter the enforcement of those rules, the faster students can learn them, and the less severe the consequences of misbehavior need to be. The trick is to give the enforcement as little energy as possible. All the energy and relationship are saved for when the rules are not being broken!

The bulk of this book discusses practical techniques that energize success. These techniques enable you to use your valuable relationships to encourage students to ever-greater heights of success. This book also contains plenty of concrete guidance on how to enforce rules. As you read, however, keep in mind that these are *methods* leading to the ultimate goal of this book—building inner wealth—and not ends unto themselves.

## The Ultimate Goal: Building Inner Wealth

The ultimate goal of this book is to transform who students think they are, the life they think they will have, and to give them abundant evidence that they are valuable, good, competent, and able to cope well with life. In the nomenclature of the Nurtured Heart Approach, we say that the goal of the approach is to create inner wealth within students.

Inner wealth enables children to use good judgment, make good choices, resist exploitation, choose good partners and friends, think of the future, cope with adversity, take risks, and find courage and love. Are we talking about "self-esteem?" Yes, but self-esteem is only one part of inner wealth. Inner wealth is much broader, deeper, and more resilient.

Too often, adults try to convince children to have greater self-esteem by giving them a pep talk about how terrific they are—often, in response to some kind of adversity. This is not what we do in this approach. Self-esteem, in this model, is instilled through an accumulation of first-hand experiences of *actually being held in esteem for successes that are pointed out in real time and in poignant ways.*

Seems obvious, but this isn't how we have been taught to look at the self-esteem issue. When talking about this subject with an adult colleague, she laughed. "I remember how, during my most troubled teen years, my supposedly forward-thinking parents would yell, 'Your problem is that you don't have any *self-esteem!*' Like it was something I was supposed to just *have,* like clean fingernails and good grades, and it was my fault if I didn't have it!" A person's inner wealth determines how well he will cope with low self-esteem, damaged self-esteem, or even with super-high self-esteem.

It is this inner wealth, gained from social interactions, that your students will pass on to their own children. The most pivotal social curriculum children receive comes first from communication between parents and children and second from their school environment. It's not unrealistic to say that teaching in a manner that expands children's sense of inner wealth could dramatically improve lives for generations to come. And, in the here and now, it helps students focus and achieve better in the classroom.

This is what Lounsbury refers to as the "hidden curriculum." There is an academic curriculum *and* a process curriculum; the latter teaches the students who and what they are. The Nurtured Heart Approach helps identify and codify this process curriculum to help you communicate and optimize your expectations and standards for each and every student.

Let's look in more detail at some of the basic foundations of the Nurtured Heart methodology. In the first book describing the Nurtured Heart Approach, *Transforming the Difficult Child,* the approach is presented in detail for parents who need new tools for parenting their intense children. Here, we expand and refine that information specifically for teachers and administrators.

## Creating Experiences of Success

When we implement the Nurtured Heart Approach in the classroom, we are strategically creating actual *experiences of success* for children within the context of their activities and relationships.

Most people are fluent in the language of failure. We can talk for hours about what is going wrong, spinning suspenseful and entertaining drama as we go. Perfectionists and cynics fit into our culture much better than the individual who is all about finding the good in things. Consider our consumer culture, which aggressively tries to instill a sense of lack, need, and falling short in order to persuade us to buy things—and children are especially vulnerable to those messages.

In general, people do not naturally accentuate the positive. When we do, we tend to spout positivity in ways that are disingenuous or "Polyanna-ish." Most of us are deeply indoctrinated to squash negativity through fear, threats and punitive actions and sigh a quiet breath of relief when the negativity temporarily goes away.

When the negative behavior stops, we fail to acknowledge its replacement behaviors with anything close to the same level of enthusiasm, if at all. *That's what she should have been doing all along*, we think.

Traditional teaching, like traditional parenting, energizes unwanted behavior by giving it stronger, more animated and more vivid acknowledgement than is accorded the behaviors that are desired. The majority of your focus and effort are expended on teaching the lesson and smoothing any ripples of misbehavior. When you say, "I'm waiting for quiet," the room is in the hands of one or more noisy children ready to rev you up for a major mood disorder. A student makes a funny noise, many laugh, and now the class receives an intense lecture on how bad and unproductive they are. Some students quiet down, but the intense relationship-seeker ("difficult student") laughs at you or even insults you.

In this situation, by relying on traditional disciplinary approaches, you have inadvertently deepened the child's impression that he gets more out of adversity than through good choices. In essence, this is like handing the student a hundred-dollar-bill for making a poor choice. No one would do this on purpose, of course, but we do it accidentally all the time.

Ultimately, you may have to send this student to the office. He moves on to another version of the same reactions with an administrator: sit quietly, receive a lecture with warnings, and maybe get booted to In-School Suspension. The student goes home and gets the sequence again, or perhaps nothing happens. Anyway, tomorrow is a new day, and with so many ways people can be annoyed, your student is sure to continue seeking more intense relationships through problematic behaviors. After all, the relationships he forms are loaded with drama and excitement, even if they are markedly unfulfilling. He wards off that feeling of unfulfilled desire for connection by creating some more excitement (i.e., difficulty). Most importantly, the student has a high level of control when he is creating these negative relationships. It's easy and he can do it whenever he feels like it—and can, by and large, count on getting the same energized responses over and over.

**With the Nurtured Heart Approach, fulfilling relationship is consistently offered.** The difference is that the excitement, drama, and attention occur in response to *good* qualities. This student and every student will come to recognize success as their only option.

Some children—and you know which they are—wind up getting a lot of negative attention. They accumulate life experiences of failure. The interventions of the Nurtured Heart Approach are designed to give these children experiences of success so they can begin to accumulate a positive portfolio of who and what they are, of others, and of the world.

This is accomplished by a combination of:

- **Relentlessly reflecting ongoing successes back to the child;**

- Strictly enforcing limits; and

- Repeatedly demonstrating to children that they cannot extract negative relationship and energy from you by causing problems.

We call this the "three-legged table," and without any one of the three legs, it topples. You will read a great deal more about this table and how to keep it standing in chapters to come.

Success is powerful medicine. There is no greater evidence of this than the response of the child who feels successful even when limits are being set for her—and this is how a child can feel when adults use this approach in the classroom or at home.

## Our Energy and Relationship Are Our Greatest Gifts

Howie Glasser arrived about a half-hour before the end of the day at a school where he was presenting an in-service program for teachers. He was in one area of the library setting up his equipment. Nearby, children worked independently on their projects at several large round tables, and two teacher-librarians were at their console at the front of the room. For the first 15 minutes Howie was there, no interaction took place between the teachers and children. Then a minor disruption occurred at one of the tables. One teacher immediately made her way over to the child causing it. In a clearly caring manner, she took the child aside, put her arm around him and in a kind voice urged him to stay focused and not bother the other children. Within minutes the same child was acting out again, this time accompanied by several others.

Although the teacher was obviously urging the child to make better choices, she was inadvertently rewarding him for having made the wrong choice. He got wonderful, caring, loving *relationship*. He found himself being rewarded, but was also being told to behave differently. The teacher energetically handed him a hundred-dollar bill while telling him to stop the behavior that had seemingly earned it. Other children saw this clearly and decided to get some of that relationship for themselves. Children are masters at detecting the energetic bottom line.

That this teacher was caring and loving is not something we would ever wish to change. Many of us can now recall a time when disciplinary approaches involved far less gentleness and much more harshness. But harsh approaches gain order in the moment at the expense of children's long-term mental and physical well-being. In the situation recounted above, it is the teacher's *timing* that leaves everything to be desired. What she needs to do is shine that caring guidance and appreciation on her students *when rules are not being broken*.

This may sound like an awful lot of work and time, and if you're already overwhelmed, you may feel tempted to put this book aside and forget about it. But it *doesn't* take more time than putting out disciplinary fires. It takes less time. When we implement the Nurtured Heart Approach with parents, their intervention with their child typically amounts to something like five minutes a day. That's enough to transform a child *when the interventions are done correctly.*

So, if you are in an elementary school, a few minutes per day per child might amount to slightly more than an hour of classroom time. In secondary schools, all you need is about five minutes per class period. Keep in mind that, in the classroom, all eyes are on you and the way you interact with every student. Even when you do not directly address each and every student, they still see and experience the way you respond to others, and they soon realize that your energy and relationship will come to them more readily when they are doing the right things.

## The Nurtured Heart Approach is the Selective and Loving Management of Relationship

When people we are very interested in approach us, our physical and mental energy quickly shifts in their direction. We want to sustain the contact—even amp it up a bit so it is even more "electric." You probably didn't initially connect to your spouse or partner or friend by waiting several moments and then slowly turning and mumbling a greeting. You probably won't stay connected, either, if you are habitually slow to acknowledge their existence and exude minimal energy toward them or exude energy only when things are going wrong.

**How we access and sustain the energy of others toward us, and how we give our energy to others, is basically what makes the world go around. Selective and loving management of this process is the Nurtured Heart Approach.**

Difficult children believe that the only way they can access this precious gift of interest and energy from others is by acting out. They get a lot of engagement with adults that may be negative and unfulfilling, but is also very compelling. Withdrawn or depressed children are manifesting their belief that they are incapable of getting the energy and relationship they need from others.

## Brave New World, Brave New Approach

Over 55,000 books have been written about methods for parenting and teaching. Almost all describe variations of normal, conventional, and traditional approaches—the same approaches currently taught to aspiring teachers in colleges and universities. Many of the professors have never been in a classroom themselves, or they were teachers so long ago that they haven't a clue about what their graduates are in for. This puts both today's teachers and today's students at risk of "dropping out." Parents and communities are put at risk as well when traditional approaches to education don't work and children spin out of control.

The widely quoted figure on student dropout rates before high school graduation is 20 percent. The real figures, depending on children's ethnicity and socioeconomic status and on whether the schools in question are urban schools in challenging areas, range from 50 percent to 23 percent.[4]

It seems obvious that we no longer have the luxury of doing things the way we've been doing them in our schools. Times have changed and we all need to be stronger on the inside. This requires a shift in perspective … reaching deeper to conjure up our wherewithal more often and at greater levels than ever before. The complexity, pressures, and stresses of today's world require a new approach—the Nurtured Heart Approach.

Normal approaches work to some extent with easy children, but our experience with thousands of people shows that normal approaches tend to backfire with children who are more intense, sensitive, or needy. If you've read the wrong 54,990 books, you're going to be in trouble when it comes to working effectively with intense and challenging children.

Children who could be characterized as intense, sensitive, or needy discover early on in the classroom and at home that they get more response from their actions when they make negative choices. They discover the truth: that poor choices lead to much more relationship, discussion, and connection, all of which they desperately crave. Good behavior, on the other hand, earns them the same tired iterations of "thank you" and "good job"—if that.

The heightened response they get when things go wrong academically or behaviorally—all that extra juice coming through the wires—makes them feel more valued for the wrong reasons, and they come to count on this. The child that fits this description comes to feel more loved and cared for when things go wrong. We can tell them the opposite all day, but what holds the most weight is the truth of our *actions*. When you begin to implement the Nurtured Heart Approach, you will see exactly what we mean.

When we take this perspective, we can abandon the blame game altogether. It isn't the teacher, or the parent, or the child who is the culprit: it's the *methods we have at our disposal.*

## How Normal Parenting and Teaching Methods Put "Good" Children at Risk

One parent who was learning the Nurtured Heart Approach told us a story that serves as a good illustration of this point:

*My five-year-old son Jason is a handful—a perfect candidate for the Nurtured Heart Approach. Before I started using it with him, he was all over the place, and it seemed he was looking for opportunities to create chaos. I could turn away and turn back five seconds later, and he'd have started taking apart the stereo or peeling the wallpaper off the walls with a kitchen knife.*

---

4. Pynkus, Lindsay, "Who's Counted? Who's Counting? Understanding High School Graduation Rates," **www.all4ed.org/publications/WhosCounting/WhosCounting.pdf**

*Keeping him out of trouble and keeping him from damaging property felt like a full-time job. My daughter Nicola, on the other hand, is two years older and an angel. Since day one, she's helped me look after her little brother. She does well in school, and she knows wrong from right and has no problem walking the straight and narrow path. One day, I was putting out fires with Jason as usual, and out of the clear blue, Nicola just broke down crying inconsolably. "What is it?" I asked her. "I don't get enough attention!" she sobbed. "You're always dealing with Jason, and you never have time for me!"*

This mom redoubled her efforts to acknowledge her daughter *and* her son when they were doing things right. Not an easy task, and not something we learn to do effectively in traditional teaching or parenting practices. With our approach, parents and teachers get the tools to continually support and enrich all kinds of children.

Good, well-behaved, high-achieving students pick up on the fact that challenging students draw more than their fair share of teacher energy, response and relationship. They're keenly aware of the inequity of this setup and are sometimes downright mad at their teachers because of it. These children want and deserve celebration and closeness, too! Unfortunately, because teachers feel forced to deal with problems first and spend most of their energy doing so, these children can end up experiencing the classroom as a no-win environment.

And then there are the marginal children: those who are on the borderline. They are watching adults very carefully and constantly observing what other children do to earn energy and focus from adults. These children could go either way. If consultants are called into the classroom as per a challenging child's Individual Education Plan (IEP), the end result typically is that even more positive statements and encouragement (i.e., energetic hundred-dollar bills) are directed to *only* the challenging child. The good children become even angrier and the marginal children are drawn inexorably toward the clear advantages of being "difficult." So many IEPs backfire; we believe that methods that inadvertently energize failure are to blame.

Fortunately, the Nurtured Heart Approach works for high achievers as much as it does for children who present significant challenges, and it helps marginal children go in the right direction. And unlike IEPs, this approach is designed to work as a whole-class intervention, not just for difficult children.

## Inner Wealth Helps Students Stay Safe

Across the U.S., schools are making a concerted effort to help students choose not to smoke cigarettes or use drugs and alcohol. We expose children to programs that educate them about these substances and their detrimental effects. We alert them to the pressures they may face; many schools role-play those scenarios to prepare them for the day when it's their turn to "Just Say No." Many schools also offer health education so students will learn how to avoid pregnancy and sexually transmitted diseases.

A child who has taken these classes but who lacks a sufficient level of inner strength is overwhelmingly likely to say *yes* in the face of pressure to smoke, drink, get high, or have sex. (To be fair, many of these programs try to instill inner wealth or self-esteem in children, too—it is so obviously an essential ingredient of the "just say no" mix—but the Nurtured Heart Approach creates a higher order of inner wealth than these other programs.) On the other hand, a child who hasn't been exposed to these programs but who possesses a significant level of *inner wealth* is in a more advantageous position when it's in her best interest to say no. Such a child has more resources to draw upon. Even if saying no is a struggle, she can conjure up whatever it takes. And if she does slip up and make a mistake, she is more likely to recover and bounce back from it.

For the sake of all children who are at risk with normal approaches—and the teachers and parents entrusted with their care—we need a method that solves the riddle of intense children *and* helps all the other children flourish. Such a method leads a child to perceive an inner sense of greatness, which makes him more likely to act from that inner sense than he would if living under the shroud of negativity.

We believe that the Nurtured Heart Approach has proven itself to be such a method. With this book, we hope to convince you of the same.

# Chapter Two

## *Getting Started: Setting the Conceptual Foundation*

THE METHODS WE USE in the Nurtured Heart Approach are based on varying levels of celebratory praises of the child's character, heart, and spirit: the sum of his or her inner wealth. The child's behavior naturally evolves into a reflection of his or her belief in that inner wealth. We show children that they are worth celebrating, no matter what, and sooner or later they come to accept that they can be—that they *are*—successful.

**This approach is *not* about "B-S-ing" our students, or sugar-coating what is actually bad behavior** (which we all know doesn't work, because they see right through it); **it is not about being disingenuous or untruthful.** It is crucial to remain constantly grounded in the reality of the moment, in whatever we are seeing and experiencing in the classroom, and finding something to celebrate about what's going on. It's about seeing the cup as half full rather than half empty. And we are additionally empowered when we develop techniques to create situations where children can't help but be successful.

The Nurtured Heart Approach doesn't even really measure the glass as half full or half empty. It isn't "wow, you're half a glass of water!" or "wow, you're on your way to being a full glass!" or even "wow, you've lost half your water, but you've still got some beautiful hydration left." Instead, it's "wow—you're some *sparkling* water!" Feel the difference?

One of Howie Glasser's favorite illustrations of this "half-full" mindset is the story of a driver on his morning commute across the Oakland-Bay Bridge. As the driver nears the tollbooths and rolls down his window, he hears loud rock-and-roll dance music. He sees a tollbooth attendant a few lanes away, grooving to the beat and having a great time. Traffic is light, so he's able to move into that toll taker's lane. As he pulls in, the driver says to the attendant, "It looks like you're having the time of your life." The tollbooth attendant answers: "Of course! I have the best job in the world and the best office in the world."

"Really?" The driver has never thought of taking tolls on the Bay Bridge as an occupation to be sought after. The toll taker goes on: "Sure! I get to be out here, listening to my favorite tunes, meeting nice people, doing my own thing. Besides— what executive do you know who has an office with four glass walls and a view that even comes close to this one? I can look west and almost see the ocean; north and south, I get beautiful views of the bay; and there to the east I see the mainland.

On the early shift, I get to see the sunrise. On a later shift, I get to watch the sun set. The view is different every day with all the clouds moving around. Besides— I'm a dancer, too, and I'm getting paid to practice!"

The driver then gestures toward the other tollbooths. "What about the other attendants? They don't seem to be having the time of their lives." To which the attendant responds: "Oh—those guys in the stand-up coffins? They're no fun."

*Everything is subject to how we choose to see it.* We have the privilege of being able to choose the way we look at things. No other creature on the planet has the brainpower to do this. We can adopt a loving and positive attitude—as the dancing toll taker did—or we can think of our cup as half empty, dreading another day of pollution, noise, traffic, and headaches.

Moment to moment, we get to make that choice. Even if we've spent every moment up until now being negative, cynical, and angry, we can choose, in this very moment, to see things differently. The Buddhist spiritual teacher Thich Nhat Hanh tells us to *just smile.* "How do we smile when we feel angry or sad?" we might ask. He would answer that we are not only our sadness, not only our anger. We can choose to smile at those feelings, too.

Circumstances do not have to change, nor do we have to ignore the truth of our circumstances. We can point our camera and take a photograph that reflects absolutely the reality of what we are seeing, and we can find the positive in that. Even on the most dismal city street, tiny plants push up through the pavement, and someone along that stretch of road is being kind, experiencing joy, or helping someone else.

How does this apply to the Nurtured Heart Approach? It illustrates the way in which we can train ourselves to see and acknowledge the positive and the good instead of the negative when we are in the classroom. It is admittedly harder to do on some days than others. Sometimes, it can feel forced. But each moment offers another chance to choose to nurture instead of control the students to whom you are so important.

The story of the toll taker illustrates the foundation of this approach. Creating success where it does not normally exist, and fixing your mind to seek out success in the apparently mundane, are essential skills and intentions that will let you be thrilled with your situation just like the toll taker.

## Beginning to Catch and Create Successes in the Classroom

Even the child with the most intense, rapid-fire negative behavior can be "caught" being successful in some small way. However, the main problem with trying to "catch" a child being good is that we can end up waiting for something to strike us *as good enough to be worthy of comment.* Our approach is all about "creating" goodness and acknowledging that goodness to the child in simple, effective, targeted ways. That is all it takes to plant the seed of change that will, with continued effort on the part of caring adults, eventually transform the child.

The types of comments used in the Nurtured Heart Approach to "create" goodness or success fall into two basic categories:

- We can give children a reflection of what they *are doing* or what they *have done*. We can then specifically reflect how they are being successful in those actions—actions that typically seem very common or mundane. For example:

  > "I notice that you are creating a pattern with the colored tiles. You're staying really focused. I see how determined you are to line up the edges and to alternate colors."

  > "I see that you've pitched in with the others to clean up the art area. That's very considerate and responsible. Thank you, your efforts are appreciated."

- We can point out undesirable things they are *not doing* as examples of success in the moment. Here, too, we point out why their choices to avoid negative behaviors are making them a success.

  > "I so appreciate that you haven't been teasing the other kids at your table this morning. You're showing great self-control!"

  > "You are so frustrated and you didn't take your frustration out on anyone or anything. You're using powerful self-control."

**Often, people who are learning this approach jump in here and say, "Oh—so you mean I need to *catch* the child doing good." In practice, the Nurtured Heart Approach is different, especially with extremely difficult children. We have to *create* a situation where the child basically is hijacked into success.**

One example we like to use is that of the child who has been out of control all day, and Mom comes to pick him up from school. She knows it's been tough for him. When they get to the car, she hands him her purse and says "Here, hold this while I open the door," *without giving him time to think about it*. Once the door is open, she says, "I really appreciate your holding my bag. Thank you for helping out." This might be the first positive thing he's heard all day, and it could be the first step toward turning things around for this child.

This approach relentlessly and proactively focuses on the good already there— *even in the midst of "bad" behavior that is often present when this intervention is initially started with a child*. It assumes that something good is always going on at some level and requires that we point out this goodness via positive reflections. **We are not leaving it up to the child to decide to be totally good; we are surprising the child with the success and wonderfulness she possesses before she has time to even realize it. We do this even when she is having a problem in ways that expand the** child's understanding of herself. **Thus, we are not "catching children being good,"** nor are we focused solely—or even primarily—on "good" behavior. We are proactively focusing on and expanding the goodness of a child's spirit and character; and there are times we do so regardless of what's going on at the moment with the child. In reality, something good is almost always occurring. The key is to learn to find and acknowledge those instances.

For example, let's say Tonya is being disruptive during a class activity by cutting in front of others to grab supplies and talking and goofing around while the class is trying to complete the activity. She'll need a brief time-out/reset because she is breaking at least one rule. In fact, to be as strict as you need to be per the Nurtured Heart Approach, you will give her a time-out/reset *every single time* she breaks a rule. (These time-outs/resets are only going to take a few seconds each; more on this in Chapter Five.) But once she's completed her time-out (and been praised for doing so successfully), then it's time to create "time-in" as quickly as possible. You might do this by noticing and acknowledging that she is being creative in the way she uses the materials: "Tonya, I see that you're using the cut straws and tissue paper in a really unique way to build a tall tower. That shows great focus and creativity!" Absolutely resist the temptation to add something like, "Now, if you could only keep your voice down and stop bothering your classmates, you'd be doing even better." The rule-breaking is in the past. She did her time-out—it's over, and it's a new moment! Find a way to point out her successes.

The practical application of the Nurtured Heart Approach will probably require a shift in your thinking in significant ways. Keep your mind and heart open to adopting a whole new paradigm—one that may feel a bit upside-down or forced at the outset. A shift in your heart, in your own inner wealth, will translate to the actions you take with your students. They'll see it in you and know it's for real, not a disciplinary trick you're using to try to control them. In fact, we do not even think of this as a disciplinary approach. Good behavior certainly is an outcome of the Nurtured Heart Approach, but it is secondary to clearly focusing on recognizing and building your students' inner wealth.

## The "Energy-Challenged" Child

You may have noticed that we have not used any kind of diagnosis to describe difficult children. At this writing, most schools, parents, and doctors lean strongly toward diagnosis when things go wrong in a child's life—Attention Deficit Hyperactivity Disorder (ADHD), Oppositional Defiant Disorder (ODD), depressive disorders, anxiety disorders, or a combination. Although we are not psychiatrists, we can say with a great deal of confidence that these diagnoses and the drugs prescribed to "treat" them have reached ridiculous heights of overuse. The incidence of ADHD diagnosis has risen to encompass five to 10 percent of American children. No other nation comes even close to this level of diagnosis and drugging of the pediatric population.

We believe that the Nurtured Heart Approach is a viable alternative to drug treatment for children who have been "diagnosed" with ADHD, ODD, or others related to problem behavior. The approach also is extremely effective with the "average" child.

Countless times, we have seen parents at the end of their tether, believing that drugs—and their accompanying side effects and long-term hazards—were the only option for their children. Through the Nurtured Heart Approach, these same parents were able to enjoy wonderful transformations in their relationship with the child that made drugs unnecessary. In rare instances, children *will* need pharmacological or therapeutic help regardless of the best efforts of educators and parents; but we know that literally thousands of children who might otherwise be diagnosed and drugged can be helped with this approach alone.[5]

For now, let's forego diagnoses and labels and examine what we have found to be the common denominator for so many "ADHD" children and others with intense dispositions or difficult behaviors: energy. More specifically, the intense or difficult child is an energy-challenged child.

This means that the child has trouble controlling and directing his energy. Some energy-challenged children have abundant energy: they might be hyperactive, aggressive, extremely needy, or act out, for example. Others seem to have not quite enough energy: the withdrawn, depressed, or anxious child could fit this description. The seemingly low-energy child may have given up getting what he needs; he may have plenty of energy, but may have made the choice to suppress it.

Some children are blessed with such abundant energy that they seem to be able to cause three kinds of trouble at once. It requires huge effort for them to channel that abundant energy. We like to use the analogy of trying to stop a tractor-trailer with old Model-T brakes. Most of us cannot even begin to appreciate how hard this can be for the child. She may actually already have more control than the average child—but it's not nearly enough to handle what's going on inside her.

We can provide tools to help her move all that wonderful energy in a direction that will help her feel successful and happy rather than always being in trouble and creating disruptions and problems wherever she goes. We do so by showing that child that *our* energy—which she needs and desires—will come to her not in response to acting-out or bad behavior, but in response to positive qualities and behaviors. And through this new response, we show the child that *her energy is the source of her great actions and choices.* These new experiences of success become

---

5. For a very detailed analysis of the physical and psychological hazards of drugs commonly used to treat ADHD and other childhood behavioral issues, refer to Howie Glasser's book, *101 Reasons to Avoid Ritalin Like the Plague,* available at amazon.com and at **www.difficultchild.com.** We also recommend the writings of Peter Breggin, M.D., a psychiatrist who specializes in the hazards of prescription psychiatric drugs like Prozac and Ritalin; visit **www.breggin.com** for titles of his books and to read some of his insightful articles.

internalized and contribute to her growing portfolio of becoming a successful person.

It's not that we ignore bad behavior; later on, you'll learn simply to mete out consequences for that behavior in a highly predictable and *un-energized* way. You can start today to think about this. How much of your energy gets poured into responding to problems? Do you raise your voice and show your frustration when dealing with those problems? Do you talk and talk and talk to the child who's out of line, hoping somehow that this lecture will be the one where he finally *gets* it? If you are doing any of these things, you are handing over your most precious and valued commodity—your energy—to children when they are doing wrong. It's an upside-down approach, and you'll learn in this book how to turn it right-side-up.

## The Element of Adult Energy

Both over-energized and under-energized children crave and desire the energy that comes from adults during interaction. They are all trying to find their way in the world and to learn to feel successful. They want to *belong*. They know intuitively that maintaining connection and focus with an adult is the way to learn how to manage their own energy better. They know that they need this connection and focus to learn how to survive and thrive in the world. Sometimes they just don't know how to get or maintain that energetic link.

When a child gets his entire daily share of adult energy and relationship when he's being "bad" and virtually none when doing what he's supposed to do, what do you think he's going to decide is his best route toward satisfying his need for that energy? The answer is obvious: he's going to be "bad."

One reason why life stays so unmanageable for the energy-challenged child are the approaches traditionally used to try to help such children rein themselves in. These approaches pay little attention to the child who's "behaving" and rain down all manner of focus, lectures, reprimands, and other highly energized forms of communication on the child who isn't.

Although lectures, reprimands, and punishments don't sound like much fun to most of us—and even the child who seems to crave them would probably say he would rather avoid them entirely—the energy-challenged child can't seem to help but go back to that place again and again. *They need the connection more than they fear the negativity.*

## We Are Children's Favorite "Toys"

Adults are, in essence, children's favorite toys. We are unique among toys in that we can interact with, connect with, and nurture the children.

Toys are getting ever more complex, with possibly hundreds of features, sounds, lights, and complicated instructions. Children go for the complicated toys with lots of interesting features. But *even if they had a thousand features, these toys could not begin to approach the number of amazing features possessed by a human being.* Important adults are, by far, children's favorite "toys." We're loaded with features and we're animated, reactive, and interactive. We also have the best remote control ever made.

In addition to our ability to walk, talk, skip, dance, wax poetic, make faces, and do just about anything else under the sun, we can display a multitude of fascinating emotions and moods in a virtually infinite number of combinations, subtleties, and gradations. Our actions and feelings can be paired in so many ways: one day, the teacher writes a lesson on the board with lots of happy flourishes and silly comments that make his students giggle; another day, he writes a lesson on the board with a foul mood emanating through every gesture and word.

No other "toy" could possibly compete. To children, adults are personal entertainment centers, more interesting than any other toy. Our volume buttons are readily displayed, and other buttons beckon to be tried out by children just to see what will happen. When the right buttons get pushed in the right sequence, that *really* can get the show going!

These "buttons" are irresistibly fascinating to the sensibilities of children who are actively forming opinions about how the world works and about their place in it and effect upon it. They see very early that their manipulations of this toy will yield differing levels of energy, interaction, and connection.

Now, let's imagine that a child in your classroom is slow to move to his seat when it's time. You're in a rush to get to the lesson, and he's goofing around, showing no intention to do what you've asked. You might respond by expressing some annoyance or frustration: "Charlie, would you *please* get to your seat?" This is a standard, mainstream method of getting a child to fall in line, using words like "please" and trying to ask nicely despite your obvious frustration.

If he still does not respond, you might move to more animated instructions, warnings, or threats of consequences. Stern lectures and reprimands may come next. With the average child, these approaches usually work in the end. In any case, the child gets an illustrative and comprehensive view of how to get the "toy" (i.e., you) to have a more animated reaction. **The child IRREFUTABLY sees that the toy is much more reactive and energized when adversity strikes.**

This observation becomes even more crucial in the case of an intense, sensitive, or needy child who wants and needs your energy so badly that she's willing to weather your negativity. She sees that adults exhibit so much more "NO" energy than they do "YES" energy and readily becomes convinced that the payoff is greater for *not* doing what is asked of her. The relatively neutral level of acknowledgement that children usually receive when they're "good" can't match the energy they witness when adults jump all over failures. Intense, sensitive, or needy children see how non-success captivates adults, drawing our focused attention and eliciting bigger reactions.

Even the most common teaching anthem of "catching the child being good" tends to leave us in a disempowered position with the challenging child because we are merely waiting for something that catches our eye before making a positive comment—one that typically pales in comparison to all that transpires when things go awry.

Some traditional methods for dealing with discipline issues refer to difficult children as more attention-seeking. With the Nurtured Heart Approach, we view it to be more about *reaction* than attention—the payoff is the *level of energy* or *level of response* that the child comes to expect in response to various events. It's not just attention, but *energized* attention: the relationship, the connection, and the bigger "dose" of perceived love that flows when things are going wrong. The child sees again and again that "being good," having a positive attitude, or not breaking the rules nets less response. He goes for the bigger slice of life every time.

The Nurtured Heart Approach aims to make better behaviors much more energetically rewarding than out-of-line behaviors. That's how we turn the energy equation right-side-up.

This is not to say that the average child can't be wonderfully guided when exposed to the Nurtured Heart Approach. Every child will feel enriched as the classroom becomes a more positive place. No more will you have to spend so much valuable time dealing with troublemakers, causing the better-behaved kids to feel left out. You will have time to hand out positive reflections to every child in the room—and maybe a few to yourself and your co-workers while you're at it!

Generally speaking, children see adults as the most competent, intelligent, knowledgeable, and powerful people imaginable. An adult can bestow enormous value, honor, and worth to a child, and we hold most of the cards needed to access whatever children want. In the eyes of children, adults are usually seen as wise and able to remedy any situation. Remember how shocked you were when you found out that your parents didn't know everything?

Imagine the difficulty children have when this most spectacular and wise toy becomes baffled, loses control, and tells the child that he is to blame for that misery and distress. The child has discovered that he is more influential over the adult than the adult is over himself or herself. He finds once again that there is more intense relationship through routes of adversity.

The Nurtured Heart Approach shows children that they cannot deregulate the most powerful, valuable toy on the planet; that there is more energetic relationship to be had through success; and that adults can lead them into ever higher levels of joy as the game of life goes on.

## Accomplishing Transformation with the Three-Legged Table

In Chapter One, we mentioned the "three-legged table" of the Nurtured Heart Approach. The analogy is meant to remind you that you must apply all three elements of the approach or it won't work. The three factors that successfully transform a classroom rely upon one another. Like a three-legged table, if one leg goes, it doesn't matter how strong the other two are: the table will topple.

Now we will describe the legs of the table in more detail.

1. **Relentlessly reflect ongoing successes back to the child.** *Resolve to purposefully create and nurture successes and positivity; relentlessly and strategically draw students into new and renewed patterns of success.*

This is the heart of building inner wealth for the children in your classroom. Be like the mirror in that one fitting room in your favorite clothing store that makes you look spectacular. That reflection of you isn't a lie, no matter how you look in the mirror at home; it is the truth about you in that moment! Reflect back to students their most beautiful selves. Pursue the positive. This is what the techniques presented in the chapters that follow are designed to do, and we know from experience that they work. They expand inner wealth and self-esteem and ultimately change people's ways of moving through life.

2. **Strictly enforce rules.** *Have clear rules and clear, consistent, effective consequences when those rules are broken.*

Too often, classrooms try to couch rules in vague positive language. "Be responsible"…"Cooperate"… "Have good manners"… "Play nice!" This kind of language suggests that the students already know what these concepts mean and can navigate appropriate behavior without more specific instructions. This is indeed the case with most children. With that significant few who can derail a classroom, however, more specific rules are necessary. Presenting those rules more specifically won't hurt the other children in your classroom, so everyone benefits.

It might be tempting to levy warnings or threats on the spot. "If you don't finish your assignment, you won't go out for recess." "If you keep talking out of turn, you won't be going to the computer lab today." With those who are over-energized, this method usually backfires and escalates into a series of tests and threats. With very under-energized children, this method often does no more than elicit a "so what?" or "who cares?" posture.

Consequences must be clear, predictable, consistent, and always followed through when working with over- and under-energized children. We will have lots of advice about how to make effective consequences, but the most important aspect of creating consequences that actually work is to combine them with a firm and broad foundation of positivity and success. Once we stop energizing problems, children recognize that doing what's right is an option that reaps much greater response than acting out or causing problems. At that point, consequences may be as simple as an extremely brief "reset." (More on this in Chapter Five.)

Enacting consequences without supplying the foundation of positivity will not work, at least not in the context of the Nurtured Heart Approach. They're two halves of a whole that won't work without one another.

3. **Consistently demonstrate to students that they cannot extract negative relationship and energy from you.** *Refuse to get drawn into giving the child greater responses, more animation, and other unintended "payoffs" for negative behaviors. Do your best to avoid accidentally fostering failures and rewarding problems with your energy.*

Children who receive a generous dose of words of wisdom when they do something wrong often come to hate the lectures, but they love the intimacy and closeness that transpire under those circumstances. Although those messages are meant to inspire good choices, children interpret lectures as evidence of their failures. Of course, we don't mean to foster failure; still, most adults accidentally fall into this trap often. The result is that many children accumulate enough of these experiences to make them defensive against the positive statements that characterize the Nurtured Heart Approach—at least at first.

When you encounter a child who initially resists your attempts to create success, you may be tempted to revert to old methods that leak negativity. Try to see a child's resistance to your positive statements as a challenge to topple that wall by bringing forth even more success. Don't fall back into the trap of handing out hundred-dollar bills for negative behaviors. Adamantly do what it takes to make success a reality for that child.

This leg of the table is fairly self-explanatory in concept, but in practice it can be the biggest challenge. Everyone "leaks" negativity from time to time, but you can plug those leaks easily once you know how to identify them. We devote an entire chapter to "famous leaks" with examples of negativity that can undermine the application of the Nurtured Heart Approach.

Now that you have a fairly firm grasp of the theoretical underpinnings to this approach, we move on to the practical applications. First, you will learn how to provide powerful appreciation, recognition and acknowledgment for your students in ways that will transform your classroom.

# Chapter Three
## *Giving Effective Praise*

BEFORE WE GET INTO TECHNIQUES, we entreat you to remember that there is a learning curve to all this for you, the teacher. Some teachers become world-class in no time flat, but the majority take a while to get the hang of this approach. You may make your share of mistakes and from time to time leak negativity like a punctured hose. Your three-legged table will wobble; at times, it may crash to the floor. Don't worry! You can always fix it!

As you seek out positives and instill inner wealth in your students, make sure you don't berate yourself for not applying the techniques exactly right. Create inner wealth and find positives in yourself, too. As long as you have the basic concepts down, and as long as you've experienced that enlightening moment when you see that it's time to stop handing students hundred-dollar bills every time they break a rule, you can get back on track. Avoid giving energy to negativity; enforce rules strictly; and re-institute your foundation of positive praise. Voilá—your table is standing again!

If you are committed to learning this approach, keep putting yourself back on track. Like any model, it's something to be fine-tuned to suit you most comfortably. There's no single way to do this, and we love to see how the model evolves as it is used by more and more parents and teachers.

Now consider another point: the teachers (and parents) who are most successful with this model are the ones who adopt it lock, stock, and barrel. They let go of every other approach they've ever used, and they implement this one to the absolute hilt. Parents, teachers and even whole schools can become zealously attached to certain philosophies or models learned from a book, a workshop or elsewhere, and parts of it seem to truly work so well—but overall, your classroom may still need something more. And staying loyal to pieces of other approaches that conflict with this new way of thinking will inevitably make the Nurtured Heart Approach less effective.

**The teachers who do best with this approach are the ones who make the cleanest break from previous methods.** And we strongly urge you to avoid a gradual transition into this approach. It may be a shock initially for your students to have things change so dramatically, but trust us—they get on board and shift gears quite rapidly if you commit to the shift yourself.

**Once the approach is up and running and you thoroughly understand its nature,**

you can even invent your own techniques to support it; some may well be based on approaches you've used before. Bring in whatever elements help you energize success.

## Time-Out and Time-In

The time-out is considered to be an important tool for both educators and parents. It is a gentle, non-violent way of administering consequences for unacceptable behaviors. Some may think that the time-out only works for children who are already easy to manage, yet it can be a powerful element in transforming even the most disruptive child. What creates the time-out's effectiveness is its counterpart—a powerful time-in.

Simply defined, time-in is the effective recognition of success. And under the Nurtured Heart Approach, time-in essentially is in effect whenever the child is not in a time-out. It is the child's new and growing sense that she no longer has to break rules to elicit involvement but instead experiences that involvement through exposure to psychologically and emotionally nutritious comments.

Many people who have tried using time-out have been discouraged about how ineffective it can be until they started using time-in. Here's the reason: without the time-in, a time-out can easily wind up being another way of throwing hundred-dollar bills at children for their continued acting-out. In this chapter, we'll look closely at the types of positive recognition needed to power the time-in.

The aim of the Nurtured Heart Approach is to instill inner wealth in all children. "Normal" ways of parenting and teaching are completely upside-down in that problems get abundant, energized relationship and success gets very little relationship. This approach goes even further by creating moments of success where they may not otherwise occur. Relentless pursuit of the positive creates a compelling, relationship-based time-in.

The time-in happens when there is positive relationship between teacher and student. Experiencing the time-in quickly teaches children that seeking relationship through problems is unnecessary—and gives the time-out a lot more impact. As your students reap the benefits of their growing inner wealth, time-ins will be the norm and time-outs will increasingly be the exception.

In essence, the time-in is the wellspring of the child's inner wealth. It serves as a powerful social curriculum, as well as a foundation for better academic achievement. Once a child knows that there is more than enough positive relationship to go around, he begins to trust and accept that he is wonderful from the inside out and that he will be recognized for his wonderfulness and not for negative, acting-out behaviors. We all want recognition; it's sad when the juiciest versions of recognition come by way of negativity. The last thing we ever want is for a child to perceive he is most celebrated for adversity, but it accidentally happens all the time.

## Creating the Time-In

The time-in is where students:

- have specific evidence that they are good inside;
- come to feel that they have special meaning to themselves and to others;
- feel as though they belong in class;
- are confident that they are valuable to others; and
- feel competent at life management.

These good feelings are engendered through the specific appreciation, recognition and acknowledgment they receive and the way that their problems are given much less power and importance compared to the good qualities they exhibit.

While experiencing a time-in, students find that their problems have little or no power over the positive focus of the adults around them. They discover that the expectation of success is unshakable in the adults around them, even as they are held to a high level of strict rule enforcement. Students see how it feels to be highly respected. This touches their hearts, and they see that this kind of respect is worlds better than the negative attention they used to get. They feel ownership of these successes. They come to sense that they can have closeness and relationship in a straightforward and congruent manner. This is the time-in and it helps show them that they are truly valued and meaningful participants in the adventure that is their life.

Remember the three-legged table: unflagging positivity, strict limits, and no leaking of negativity. The time-in is the three-legged table in action.

In the Nurtured Heart Approach, students are not given second chances or reminders—because the adult assumes that the student is fully competent to master her own behavior. Such faith and positive expectations give the student great hope. This becomes a tremendously compelling—if not irresistible—force.

Of course, everyone has problems once in a while. The response to problems in this approach is to have a time-out from relationship—or, if this isn't possible, to make relationship as un-energized as possible. The more distinct the difference between time-in and time-out, the better.

For now, it is more important to focus on creating a bountiful time-in that will transform your classroom. Later in this book, there will be plenty of discussion on how to consequence, using time-outs in a way that quickly "resets" the student for further success.

Think of a basketball game. When the players are following the rules, they can stay in the game, playing and being part of the fun. When a rule is broken, there's a time-out and a penalty handed to the player who did the rule-breaking. Then the game starts again. No fanfare. No lecturing. Just an un-energized and predictable penalty before everyone jumps back into the game. This is what we want a time-out to be like, and we can't create that without the inherent excitement of returning to the game—the time-in.

## A New Definition of Praise

This chapter presents four types of praise that are valuable tools in getting the first leg of our table nice and strong. But before we proceed, let's make some important distinctions about the word "praise" as it's used in the Nurtured Heart Approach.

In this context, praise is defined as *positive, evidence-based reflections aimed at the heart and character of students.* We don't wait for students to achieve in prescribed ways—getting an "A" in every subject, maintaining perfect behavior all day long, answering questions correctly, or grabbing any other figurative carrot on a stick—before we praise them. We praise what they are, as reflected in what they do. We reflect their goodness, wholeness, and worthiness with celebration in this moment. We find positives upon which to begin to build a strong framework of inner wealth. In these pages, you'll find the terms "reflections," "recognitions," "acknowledgments," and "appreciations" used interchangeably with "praise."

These reflections/recognitions/praises link a behavioral observation of the student to a desirable quality of character or social quality. But it is important to keep in mind that the praises themselves are not what actually make this approach work. It is the fact that you are taking your time and energy to look deep into the student's heart and spirit; that you find him valuable, worthy, and good; and that you treat him as greater than his problems. Through experiences like these, students can take a tall drink from the fountain of meaning: the meaning we attribute to their actions, thoughts, words, and intentions. This is the lesson that will last for generations.

## Effective Praise: The Basics

You know by now that praise is at the heart of the Nurtured Heart Approach. What do you imagine when you see yourself praising the students in your class? Perhaps you envision yourself walking around the room, watching your students hard at work on an exercise, saying things like "Good job!" and "Thank you!" and "Way to go!" and "Excellent!" and "Wonderful!"

Now imagine asking the entire group, after you've finished heaping all this praise on them, whether they know what specifically you have been praising them for. They probably won't know. While this type of praise certainly conveys positive relationship, it is not specific enough to provide the evidence needed to build inner wealth or create a compelling level of time-in.

These basic forms of praise are vague and don't give adequate information. A higher-order, highly specific kind of praise is pivotal to this approach.

If you have very intense or challenging children in your classroom, you'll need to increase the frequency of your positive comments as well as the detail, intent, and emotion behind those comments. Having a particularly difficult child in your midst will force you to ramp up the level of the approach for all of the children in your classroom. As you read on, you'll see what we mean.

## The Basic Techniques

The techniques of the Nurtured Heart Approach build on one another. Here is a brief summary of the four types or levels of praise along with one or two examples. The rest of the chapter gives detailed explanations and instructions, with many more examples, so that you can gain a full understanding of how to apply these praise techniques in your classroom.

**Active Recognition:** Offers children a "verbal snapshot" of what we observe the child doing—no evaluation or judgment, just observation.

"I see that you are using red, yellow, and green yarn to make your weaving and I notice that you are alternating colors."

**Experiential Recognition:** Builds on active recognition, instilling values through the actual experience of the child. We create for the child in question a positive picture of a current or recently passed event and reframe it in a way that shows the child how a desirable value was reflected in that moment.

"I can see that you're putting a lot of effort into working with your group on your project. You're being a valuable team member. I appreciate how you are collaborating."

**Proactive Recognition:** Builds on the first two techniques to proactively recognize and highlight for the student when he is not breaking rules or not exhibiting his customary problem behavior. Remember that we are pursuing success; we give our energy to moments when the rule is not being violated and/or the student is behaving well. This is also a round-about way of introducing rules to students and reminding them what the rules and expectations are *while success is occurring*.

"Jane, thanks for not getting out of your seat while the rest of the class is finishing the assignment. You're showing respect for me and your classmates. I appreciate that you are following that rule."

"Bill, you are using a pleasant six-inch voice! Great self-monitoring! Thanks for not being loud or yelling."

**Creative Recognition:** Pulls the child further in the direction of success through use of simple, clear commands and bigger-than-ordinary reactions to gradations of compliance. This creates a flow of successes that would otherwise not exist.

(Timothy is in the process of sitting in his seat, past the point of reversing his action): "Timothy, I need you to sit down." (Once he's down): "Thank you for sitting in your seat when I told you to. You're helping me to get class going on time. You are so cooperative."

♥

ACH OF THESE TECHNIQUES helps create a deeply compelling time-in that will be balanced by the strictness and effective consequences that constitute time-out.

As you implement these techniques, you might feel at a loss about how to integrate consequences. Until we get to the specifics, just stick with whatever you have customarily done—probably some form of time-out or removal of privileges. For the time being, eliminate as much energy out of your delivery and follow-through of those consequences as you possibly can. Many find that merely giving positive recognitions like the ones above starts to produce change. Remember, though, it takes all three legs of the table to really sustain a powerful platform of change.

## Show Appreciation for Even the Smallest Effort

The famous performing orca whale, Shamu, was trained to leap over a rope suspended over his pool. How on earth did his trainers teach him to do this trick?

It started with a rope at the bottom of the pool. All Shamu had to do was swim over it to get his reward (excitement, energy, and relationship). The first few times, he more than likely swam over it by accident. When he found himself rewarded every time he happened across the rope, he put two and two together. Gradually the rope was raised, with success for swimming over the rope celebrated each time. Eventually the rope was far above the water. Shamu leaped spectacularly.

It is very much the same with your students. Each time a success is rewarded with your energy and relationship, they learn to go for that prize and receive a positive reflection of their own marvelous goodness as an additional reward. They eventually internalize the process and provide their own inner level of excitement, energy and relationship.

It is essential in this approach to look for and recognize even the smallest movements toward desired behaviors. If the child sees it as an all-or-nothing proposition where he can either succeed completely or fail miserably, his motivation to try will be greatly diminished, no matter how wonderful the reward. If Shamu's trainers had started with the rope above the pool and waited to reward him until he just happened to leap clear out of the water in a gorgeous arc over that rope, they would have had a *very long* wait on their hands. They might still be waiting!

Start thinking in terms of breaking down desired behaviors into small incremental steps, and acknowledge some of the incremental steps as successes along the way.

## A Note about Initial "Testing" Behaviors

As you begin to give praise where there was not much of it before, your students may react by resisting, acting-out, or doubting. Some, out of discomfort with this different style of interaction, may at first decide to test you in all kinds of creative ways. They may try to see whether your new attitude is for real or just a trick you are trying to use to control them. If this happens, persevere and be patient so that the students experience that there's nothing they can do to stop you from finding success and goodness in them—even if those successes or instances of goodness seem quite small.

As with Shamu's trainers, you have the advantage of an *intention* of creating successes that wouldn't otherwise exist. By way of this intention, you no longer have to feel disempowered by having to wait until you can "catch the child being good" enough to allow you to acknowledge and celebrate the positive. This intention gives you the empowered edge of seeing and creating the true successes that are emerging all the time—successes that could otherwise be missed.

Avoid criticism, lectures, admonitions, interrogations, judgments, and interpretations. As you read, you'll find more specific ideas about how to deal with students' resistance to and testing of the Nurtured Heart Approach.

## Step One: Active Recognition

The first step you will take to implement the Nurtured Heart Approach is one we call active recognition where we simply take a "verbal snapshot" of the child. We show her she's not invisible—even when she's not acting out or not doing something exemplary. You can think of this as a "video moment," where we reflect to the child exactly what we see, without any kind of evaluation or judgment.

This technique involves saying out loud what you see the child doing, almost as though you were describing it to a blind person. **Only use it when the child is doing something positive.** *Never* **do it when you see the child doing wrong.**

When you use this technique, the child knows that she is irrefutably *seen, acknowledged,* and *appreciated.* On your end, it helps you to be more attuned to noticing when the child is succeeding, or at least not misbehaving. For the child who is desperate to be noticed, recognition of her everyday actions, feelings, and expressions helps anchor her in the belief that her life really matters. It develops a foundation of trust; the child feels *seen,* her existence acknowledged. She knows she is being experienced and appreciated by others, as evidenced by the attention to detail in the statements you are making. This sets the stage for more advanced techniques as it begins to enfold students in a more positive atmosphere.

Think of it this way: we're trying to change the wiring in the child that draws him toward negativity. To change that wiring, we have to access the wire box. Active recognition is the first tool we use to do that. Below are guidelines and examples for you to follow.

**Use neutral, non-judgmental language to make the message as "digestible" as possible.**

Children who have been steeped in negativity, betrayed, or severely abused are likely to rankle at praise. Previous adults who were "nice" to them were just setting them up for exploitation. Your way around this is to start out *without* actually giving any praise; just observe and report. There's no arguing with or denying direct observations of what the child is doing or being.

**Be as specific as possible; give lots of information.**

Specificity is a key element in giving effective praise. You can say "good job" or "thank you" or "that's beautiful" with all the emotion in the world, but the child isn't going to know exactly what you mean unless you are specific. Detail makes recognition convincing to children and helps them feel cherished and validated. Active recognition gives you a chance to practice being detailed in your observations in the moment, before ever adding the element of praise. An active recognition is like a photographic opportunity to capture a moment, just the way a camera does, and to tell the truth of that moment. This technique relays that "snapshot" back to the child verbally in a way that conveys to the child that he has been successful and that he is held in esteem and worthy of your time. Self-esteem and self-worth are born from an accumulation of first-hand experiences of being valued, and this technique sets you up to create those experiences for your students.

**Examples: Active Recognition**

"Jo, I see that you are building a tower with colored blocks and you are being extremely careful, as you place them, to keep the tower balanced."

"Paul, I can tell that you are eager to go outside and play! I can see you are enthusiastic about our next activity."

"Erin, you're gluing colored paper scraps to your project. I see pink, purple, and green scraps in your pile and you're connecting them at all kinds of interesting angles."

"Jenny, I can see that you are feeling angry right now and I see you are being extremely considerate and nice by not taking it out on anyone. You are handling your strong feelings well."

Use voice modulations to put more "oomph" into your video moments.

**Active Recognition: Troubleshooting**

Children who are habituated to negative attention might tell you to knock it off when you begin to use this technique. Tom Grove has witnessed students turning, looking straight into the teacher's eyes, and saying sternly, "You have *no idea* who I am!" Don't get drawn into negativity; make it a success. Try one of these two responses:

"You may be right, but I do know [positive quality] when I see it."

Or, meet resistance head-on. You can say this to one student who resists, or to the entire class: "I realized that I've been focusing a lot on what you do wrong. Seems only fair that I notice the good things you do, too, and I hope you'll get used to it."

Some children may act out *more* when you begin to apply this technique and they begin to feel more recognized by you. This means that they want you to stay connected with them; they want you to continue the attention and recognition. They just don't quite trust the new positive connection yet. They don't know how to make the connection last without acting out. This is a wonderful sign that your positive recognition is like a bountiful banquet for very hungry people. Feed them even more! Continue to *refuse to energize negativity* and *strategically energize success*.

This technique may feel strange to you; most people were not raised in homes or schools where they were soaked in a sea of positivity on a regular basis or given such specific detail in the recognitions accorded them. Remind yourself that you are creating a comfort zone around being successful. This technique is a wonderful way to pull yourself back into the present moment and into the positive when things start to feel overwhelming.

Remember: short, sweet, positive, simple, and specific. When a consequence is necessary, issue it with as little fanfare as possible.

You can use active recognition to redirect a child before a rule is broken. But do *not* offer attention or reaction once the line is crossed. For example, you can comment on a child's handling of a tough circumstance:

"I see you are having trouble with the assignment. It's hard but you keep trying."

"I see you and your partner are disagreeing about how to proceed on the project. I see both of you trying to work it out without fighting."

"I see that you're bored and restless right now and you seem to be looking for alternative ways to stay tuned in to what the class is doing."

By offering your nurturing relationship and energy at the point before a child acts out, you are breathing life into dry moments before things fall apart. Why wait for the wheels to fall off? Then, considerably more of your time and effort will be required to clean up the wreckage. Show interest before that point. Give to the child who's about to cause trouble some information on desirable or valuable aspects of what he's doing. At the point where a rule has not yet been broken, but you suspect that it may be soon, jump in and use your "camera." You are actively using your new intentions of "toll taker" and "Shamu" to create successes that would not otherwise exist. And at the same time, you are *not* lying—just construing the larger truth with a new lens that captures successes embedded in everyday moments. Your old lens might have automatically captured the same moments but saw them as strewn with potential and emerging problems.

You can also try this technique with the adults in your life. You'll be amazed at how your colleague responds when, in the thick of an argument, you say, "I see that you are really angry at me right now…you think I should not have said what I did at the PTA meeting," instead of defending your actions and escalating the argument.

## Active Recognition: Prescription

Practice active recognition whenever you can in the classroom and in your life in general. You may not notice much change with active recognition alone. It is not transforming in itself, but it's an important skill to master, as it is really a cornerstone of this approach.

## Step Two: Experiential Recognition

In the current environment of public schools, educators often find themselves charged not only with teaching academics, but also with helping to instill constructive, positive values in students so they can become good citizens and members of society. This used to be a job relegated primarily to parents. As curricula evolve in ways designed to teach the student as a whole person rather than as a repository for facts and information, teachers are increasingly faced with expectations to reinforce value systems that help create peaceful classrooms, well-behaved students, and emerging positive citizens.

**In this step, you work with acknowledgment and appreciation in a way that helps you instill values in your students—values that can, as they are manifested, provide ever-increasing sources of positive, self-motivated behaviors for you to recognize and celebrate.**

A group of children working and cooperating well, when asked how they were being wonderful, would not say, "We're being respectful and considerate!" That's far too abstract a way for a child's mind to look at the situation. Children rarely think about their experiences in such words. They need to be taught all the behaviors that go into huge concepts like "play nicely." They need us to link what they are doing (active recognition) to the values and concepts we want them to live by.

With experiential recognition, you continue to stay in the moment and recognize the child with an active recognition, but now you expand it to include your input on which values they are showing in a positive way.

This type of recognition adds to our repertoire of techniques that empower us. By waiting for positive experiences to happen, and having a limited view of what those experiences are, we would end up in the disempowered position of hoping for just the right combination of circumstances to arise so we can say something complimentary. If Shamu's trainers had sat there with the rope high above the water, they would have been powerless. We can empower ourselves by creating "praise-able" experiences in a determined and conscious manner.

Values are defined as qualities of behavior, thought, and character regarded by a society as intrinsically good; as having desirable results that are worthy of imitation by others. They are the principles that govern behavior and reflect what is considered to be good or bad, or moral and immoral, in a culture.

Think for a moment about the values you want to teach your students. Your list might include some or all of the following:

| | |
|---|---|
| Peace | Responsibility |
| Patience | Wisdom |
| Respect | Freedom of expression |
| Friendship | Good judgment |
| Tolerance | Cooperation |
| Kindness | Good manners |
| Honesty | Compassion |
| Self control | Thoughtfulness |
| Humility | Consideration |
| Fairness | |

Unfortunately, we can talk and talk about these values to our students without really teaching them how to *live* those values. What we need to do as teachers and parents is to teach values experientially in a way that is relevant and that is an outgrowth of the child's reality.

Traditional approaches try to teach values when rules are being broken. Children are told all about the values they are *not* reflecting in their behavior. Chances are good that the child is in trouble when the lecturing happens, and she's unlikely to be at all receptive to what she is being told. She won't get the substance of your lecture (eloquent though it may be); she'll just get the confusing message of having your full attention and connection as a direct consequence of doing something she wasn't supposed to do. Energetically, we are rewarding her misbehavior...if you water weeds, the weeds will grow. And as any gardener knows, weeds don't need a lot of encouragement.

When a teacher says, "Hey, don't grab that notebook away from Jenny, that isn't very considerate of you," he or she is not helping to instill the value of being considerate. It comes across like a reprimand. The child is in a defensive state. It's a form of energizing negative behavior, which makes the issue even more likely to occur again.

Instead, we can encourage the aspects we really want to see grow: behaviors that reflect the values that are most widely accepted and respected in our society.

Here is how to apply the experiential recognition technique:

**Create a positive picture for the child of an event that is either presently unfolding or that has happened recently.**

Start with an active recognition and expand it with a comment about how what the child is doing or has done is a reflection of a value you wish to instill. "Freeze-frame" a picture of success in the here and now. Give clear, specific feedback on values, behaviors, or attitudes you consider to be desirable.

"I see that you are upset because you can't go to the computer lab with the first group. I love that you are being honest by feeling your feelings *and* being cooperative by not taking your anger out on anybody."

**Transform relatively neutral experiences into ones that are positive.**

By using common, everyday occurrences that focus on successful behaviors, you are putting the desired quality or value in the context of what the child is doing at the moment. This technique is like a video playback that heightens the child's level of perceived success. It also begins the process of defining true distinctions between desirable and undesirable behaviors, which in turn begins the preparation for effective consequences.

"Jenny, Brian, Lisa, and Tiffany, you are all working so well together. You are being wonderful by showing respect and consideration for one another."

When a difficult child is behaving well, we tend to breathe a sigh of relief and turn to other matters, thinking that we might be able to get something done while our world is peaceful. Many teachers use such moments to jump right back into the lesson. But this is your opportunity to jump in and create successes for your students; in so doing, you'll head off future problems. Propel the success even more! You'll be providing context for the desired quality and giving the child a direct experience of being held in esteem. Imagine all the quality teaching time you'll add to your day when you don't have to run around putting out fires.

The experiential recognition should express to the child that what you have seen was *exciting* to you. Other students will see your excitement and hear your recognition of the desired quality, and sooner or later they'll see that embodying that quality will earn them the precious prize of your recognition and relationship, too.

"You know, Teresa, you are being successful right now by allowing your partner to take his turn at the learning game. You are showing collaboration and generosity."

You can reflect more than character with experiential recognition. You can use this technique to reflect important "learning to learn" skills that are so essential for academic success: induction, deduction, summarizing, thinking ahead, and using prior knowledge in a present situation.

## More Examples: Experiential Recognition

"I see that you are very focused and using a lot of concentration. That's a super effort!"

"Samuel, it looks like you've used yesterday's math lesson to help you figure out today's assignment. You're applying what you learned to new challenges, and that initiative is helping you do well on this work."

"I heard you ask Alex to stop chasing you, and I see that you got really frustrated when he didn't listen. I like that you used your words first, and then that you chose to walk away. You kept your cool and didn't lash out at him. You used really good judgment and great inner strength."

"James, you're showing a respectful attitude in the soccer game. Excellent sportsmanship."

## Experiential Recognition: Troubleshooting

Remember that every desirable quality has many facets, nuances, and manifestations. A positive quality like respect or a good attitude can be reflected and recognized from many angles, each of which you can view as an opportunity to guide and nurture. You can dissect the behavior of even the worst-behaved student and find something to get excited about—even on a day when the child has been causing mayhem. Capitalize on the spaces between the mayhem and get the ball rolling by reflecting the truth of those calm moments.

When students seem to be flying right, don't assume that they know that they're doing okay; take nothing for granted. Help your students size up both new and familiar situations in a favorable light.

Here are questions we commonly hear in teacher trainings: How does the teacher avoid focusing more attention on the children who are acting up? Should the teacher shower more positivity on the difficult students, where it seems more needed, or should he or she avoid focusing more on the "difficult" children altogether?

There is real danger in putting too much energy toward shaping up challenging students at the expense of those who are generally better behaved and respectful. Give most of your relationship energy to the well-behaved students. Always pursue the positive, and that will shift the energy of the classroom, making less well-behaved students see that they will only get that coveted bit of your energy and focus from pursuing the positive themselves. At the same time, be willing to be a bit "larcenous"—opportunistically steal moments of success for all, purposefully choosing to keep the flow of successes enticing for the challenging children as well. No one is excluded from this whole-class intervention.

Resist the urge to give lessons on responsibility or self-control when the child is not using responsibility or self-control! Bringing up these qualities when they're not being exhibited ultimately winds up rewarding the behaviors we least want to energize. All the energy that goes into your lectures or reprimands is energy that ends up attached to problem behavior. Kids can come to feel that you actually love the problem behaviors. If respect and responsibility are your key concepts, teach them by poignantly describing any examples of those concepts taking place right now in the classroom.

Again, at this juncture in your application of this approach, make any consequences for poor behavior low-energy, short, and simple. Then immediately move on to pointing out the next round of success with lots of vividness and energy.

The more students vie for negative relationship, *the more the teacher responds to the students who are acting in positive ways.* By refusing to surrender the positive focus, the teacher uses the examples set by students with great behavior to show the rest of the classroom how to earn the teacher's relationship and energy. It is never necessary or okay to make comments that are intended to be hurtful, shaming, or comparative. When rules are broken even fractionally, we give a consequence designed to lead that student to future success. We relentlessly point out the successes while simultaneously refusing to energize the negative.

Be sure to remember: YOU are the treasure in the room, and YOUR relationship is more valuable than ANY the students share among themselves. Use it wisely.

## Experiential Recognition: Prescription

Apply this technique as often as possible. It begins preparation for effective consequences by defining the distinction between desirable and undesirable behaviors—again, *in the context of actual experience.* Giving a lecture on the merits of respect or reading an essay on the subject pales in comparison to demonstrating the same quality in a real-time experience where the child is essentially "accused" of being successful. Think *short, specific,* and *positive.* Be creative. Have fun with it!

Once the changes begin in your students, parents may want to know what brought them about. Teach them this technique. If you can, teach it to aides or other teachers or anyone else who has contact with your students. Consistency will make the approach work that much faster.

## Step Three: Proactive Recognition

In this step, we expand our use of the Nurtured Heart Approach to include the celebration and pursuit of success in moments where a problem is *not* occurring, or when it typically could occur. In proactive recognition, you are proactively seeking out instances where the student is not breaking a rule and you recognize the student's self-control or wise choice or good judgment in that moment.

Proactive recognition starts with you, the teacher, reexamining the rules of your classroom. We'll help you evaluate whether those rules are stated in an effective way, and if not, how to re-frame and re-introduce them to your students in a positive manner.

Typical rules in classrooms might be:

Be respectful
Keep our hands to ourselves
Follow directions

These rules are positively framed, in the spirit of positive discipline. On the surface, these rules might seem to be logical with a positive approach like this one. But that isn't the case—this is where we want negativity!

Think about the 10 Commandments. It wasn't "Thou shalt treat others with respect and gentleness," it was "Thou shalt not kill." There isn't much wiggle room there. And wiggle room is the last thing a difficult child needs. Challenging children require extremely precise rules—clear demarcations between right and wrong, acceptable and unacceptable. All children thrive when the line between "in bounds" and "out of bounds" is clear and precise. Otherwise, all kinds of border skirmishes and disagreements would take place over whether a rule has been broken or not. You yourself may even struggle to figure out whether Joey was really following directions or not, or whether Amanda was really being disrespectful. You require clarity, too, in order to zoom in and make observations about the child's successes in following the rules you have established. **Remember that every sport has very clear boundaries and rules.** The tighter the rules are, the more skilled the players must be and the more exciting the game.

Go through your list of rules and turn positives into negatives. Try a list like this one:

| | |
|---|---|
| No bad words | No getting out of your seat without permission |
| No aggression | No arguing |
| No breaking things | No name-calling |
| No talking out of turn | No teasing |

The purpose of stating the rules as negatives is *to enable you to celebrate children in your classroom for **not** breaking them.* This helps students feel thoughtful, valued, and wise just for doing what they're doing in the moment. As long as they are not doing something wrong, you can use this technique to hijack them into success. Even the "worst" student can't help but follow some of the rules, some of the time! In fact, we encourage you to create at least one rule no one ever breaks; that way, you'll always have some proactive recognition ready. Again, think Shamu and toll taker.

Here are the guidelines for giving your students proactive recognitions.

**Take a moment where a student is following the rules, freeze-frame it, then celebrate it verbally.**

**Consciously find moments when nothing seems to be happening; then, capture those moments by acknowledging students for not breaking the rules or pushing the limits in that given instant.**

**Don't concern yourself, at the outset, with having a big discussion of "the new rules" with your students.**

You can post the rules and spend a brief few minutes pointing them out, or you might suggest that the students look at them when they have a chance, instead of making them into a lecture. Often we recommend you do not have a discussion at all. We prefer you do the following:

**Surreptitiously teach the rules each time a student follows them and acknowledge the student for doing so.**

You need to know the rules cold, but they'll learn them through experience. Children do not get a new video game and dive into the rule book before playing. They load that game up and learn as they go. That's most of the fun!

Adopt a toll taker attitude to make a Shamu experience for your students!

At the instant Joshua *finally* sits down for a second after being a real wiggleworm: "Joshua, I see that you are sitting quietly in your seat and reading. It's a good choice you are making."

The child feels seen when following the rules, rather than only feeling seen when he breaks them. Actually, the child is being recognized for far more than behaving! He is being recognized for making wise decisions! This is precisely what contributes to the inner wealth aspect of this approach. Which would you prefer your boss to say: that you are an employee who knows how to behave, or an employee who is wise? The child also knows that you know the rules cold and is reassured that the boundary between positive and negative behavior is strongly drawn. You will be establishing a positive attitude about the rules instead of an adversarial relationship with them.

Difficult children think rules stink because the only time they hear about them is when they're being broken. At some point, as you apply this approach, your students will realize that *more rules are actually better,* because the more rules there are, the more time they can spend not breaking them and being recognized and praised for that.

## To Post or Not To Post?

Should you post the rules of the classroom? It's up to you. Posting rules is no guarantee that they'll be followed, and sometimes it can create a feeling of negativity—of expectation that they will be broken. Even if you do post a list of rules, don't hesitate to tell a child, "Oops, broke a rule," (and give her a time-out) for a rule that isn't on the list. You can come up with new rules anytime and add them to your list. If students protest "Hey, that's not on the list of rules," do not discuss it. Tell them they can stop by after school or the next morning if they have a question. They rarely will follow-up since what they're really trying for is some negative energy from you at that moment. As you'll learn in chapters to come, a time-out is no big deal, and breaking a rule is only a temporary reset before the student is back in the game being successful. Students learn the rules best through experience— through proactive recognition.

Keep in mind that strict enforcement of rules is one of the three legs holding this approach up. If you're going to make a rule, you must be prepared to enforce it consistently. You do so by recognizing students for not breaking it or by giving an un-energized, unemotional, brief time-out/reset when students cross that line.

## Proactive Recognition: Examples

"Brandon, I appreciate that you have not used foul language at all this morning. Thanks for following the rules."

"Jason, I like that you are not teasing the other children at your table. That's a great way to be a friend."

"Susan, I notice that you have stayed focused on reading your book for quite a while now without getting up or asking me to excuse you. Thank you for obeying the rule that reading time is about staying focused on your book."

"Tom, I love that you haven't argued with me at all while I help you with the assignment. That shows you are patient."

"Maria, I want you to know how much I appreciate that you are being so gentle with the class pet. You are showing you can really be trusted with the feelings of others."

"Franklin, you're using your power to handle your strong feelings, and you aren't being aggressive or breaking anything. That is true strength."

## Proactive Recognition: Troubleshooting

If your rules are not clear, you end up giving warning after warning as the child pushes at the boundary. This is a reward for the intense child. Positively stated rules plus unclear consequences are a surefire recipe for students to exhibit escalating patterns of testing. They are trying to find out how far they have to go to be "out of bounds," and more energy-challenged children end up with their energy bound up in bouts with confusing limits. We will talk more about making clear rules—and how to communicate them to your students—in chapters to come.

Continually look for gradations and nuances of rule adherence to help move that rope in the water higher and higher. Let's say that when the bell rings, it's time for all students to get to their seats. Peter might be horsing around or stalling in an effort to evoke an energized reaction from you. Don't go there. As long as he is moving in a positive direction and not breaking any rules, find the good in what he's doing: "Peter, I see that you're starting to move toward your seat. You're making a good choice."

**Better yet, give your praise to everyone already seated, too.** Always work to most highly energize those showing the highest standards.

Sometimes, a child will respond to this technique by blatantly and purposefully breaking a rule. He's trying to maintain the contact you've initiated. Remember the three-legged table and simply administer a non-energized consequence, moving quickly onto the next success.

Learn to use this technique to *head off* negative behavior. What's the common response when trouble is brewing? "Frances, I can tell you're about to smack Joseph. If you do, I'll send you to the principal's office!" You're basically daring the child to go ahead with the rule-breaking behavior. Instead, praise Frances for using her self-control: "Frances, I can see that you're angry at Joseph. You're using your inner strength to keep your cool and not hit or kick him. You can be very proud of yourself!"

## Proactive Recognition: Prescription

Interweave proactive recognitions with the other two techniques you're already using—active recognition and experiential recognition. Don't worry about praising too much. **You can't praise too much!!!!** Hopefully you're already seeing changes in your classroom that help motivate you to keep up the application of the Nurtured Heart Approach.

## Step Four: Creative Recognition

This technique builds on the other three to teach children to reinvest their energies successfully, constructively, productively, creatively, and joyfully. Basically, we create situations that will transport especially challenging children into success. We call it creative recognition because you are using your creativity to engineer successes that would otherwise not happen.

Every day, we ask our students to do specific things, like sit in their seats at a given time, do their work, be quiet during class time, or go to lunch or recess in an orderly way.

For the average child, a simple "All right, class has started," might be sufficient, and a low-key "Thank you" for heading to his seat might give him all the energy and relationship he needs. More intense children—the ones who are always disrupting class—need more than this. A request to do something is an easy opportunity for this child to extract energy and attention from teacher and classmates by not complying. Traditional ways of dealing with students who misbehave will earn him 100 percent of your energy every single time he refuses to do as you ask. The Nurtured Heart Approach turns this upside down. We're pulling the child further in a successful direction through the use of simple, clear commands and positive recognitions in response to gradations of compliance.

*In this type of recognition, we essentially create the compliance before the student can do otherwise!* We create a flow of successes that would otherwise not exist.

**Start with an utterly doable request. Make the request, then energize the child's response and effort.** Make the requests as simple as need be to gain compliance at some level. *Make failure impossible.*

**Avoid polite or diplomatic ways of starting out a request, like "Would you..."** or "Could you..." or "Please..."

Let's say you want your students to sit down. Don't ask them to sit, or don't use please. And by all means, don't say "You still haven't..." when a student is not doing as you say. All you're doing is heightening the child's confusion and energizing his rule-breaking behavior. (If a child doesn't sit when told to, a rule is being broken, and a time-out/reset is in order, which we cover in Chapter Five.) If you let a child get away with breaking a rule, you lose the strictness leg of your three-legged table.

**Make your requests direct, non-negotiable statements.** Say, "Everyone, I need you to sit down." As soon as anyone sits down, begin pursuing the positive and reflecting to students how they are being reliable, cooperative, and any other great quality of character you choose. Do not wait for everyone to sit before you pour out positive relationship on them.

**If you have one child who more often than not does the opposite of what you say, set aside a few instances where you can deal with him directly.**

Go near his seat and hand him your chalkboard eraser to hold while you tack something on the wall, saying "Here, hold this for a second." When he complies, thank him and offer highly specific praise. "You did a great job doing just as I asked... It shows respect and consideration."

**Remember that all of these techniques are meant to work *in the moment*. Tell the truth of this moment and leave the past and future out of it.** The child may have argued three minutes ago, and may be about to argue again, but right now, she isn't. Energize this moment, and the next and the next.

**Shift the energy to a positive spin whenever you can, conveying a message that every movement in the right direction is valued.**

This kind of reinforcement works quickly to motivate the child into doing as you ask in bigger and bigger ways. Cultivate a microscopic view of the child's successful behaviors—find and praise even the smallest successes. Increase the child's awareness of small steps, choices, and behaviors that are desirable or laudable. Keep in mind always that a child isn't going to want to run a race he thinks he can't win. The race takes this step, then another, then another. Show him how he's already making a winning step, and he'll want to get in there and run.

## Creative Recognition: Examples

When a child inadvertently tosses a block into the block bin, turn this into an opportunity for recognition and praise: "I notice that you're starting to put the blocks in the bin. I really appreciate how well you listened when I said it was time to clean up."

You've told the class that it's time for reading groups. Just as the child stands up—maybe not with the intention of walking over to his group's table—try this: "I see you walking over to join your reading group Shelly. I appreciate that you got up and are starting to do as I asked."

As a student begins to lift up his hand while holding a pair of scissors: "I need for you to hand me that pair of scissors." (The student does.) "I notice that you paid attention to what I said and handed me the scissors right away when I asked. You are very alert."

"Sam, I want you to hold this book for a second." (The student does.) "I love that you held the book just as I told you to. I noticed that you did it with a very helpful attitude."

## Creative Recognition: Troubleshooting

It's fairly common for children to resist, test, and try to either brush off your praise or actively try to pull you back into the negative patterns they have grown comfortable with. If you're being tested, return to the three-legged table. Use it like a mantra. Tell yourself: "I won't let students pull me into a pattern of failure and payoffs for negativity. I will do what it takes to pull students in the direction of success." Don't back off on the positives when students resist; if anything, turn up the dial!

Be very careful not to imply choice when making your request of students. They'll see the potential for a bigger payoff if they choose not to comply. They know from experience that not doing what they're asked to do is a great way to get the fireworks going. Simply make your request, then energize the child's response and effort toward complying. **Make failure impossible.**

If you can't resist using phrases like "good job" or "thank you," follow them up with creative recognitions.

Keep finding ways to make requests clearer and more likely to garner compliance and success. Conventional requests tend to be less clear. "I don't think it's a good idea for you to go outside without your jacket" needs to be "I need you to put on your jacket." Instead of "Why aren't you able to sit in your seat like everyone else does?" try "I want you to sit in your seat." And phrases like "When you get a chance..." or "Could you please..." are like a gilded invitation to children to not do as you would like them to do.

## Creative Recognition: Prescription

Use creative recognition for all your students to help them experience success as often as you can. It may be very helpful to begin by observing your class while an aide takes over for a moment, if that's an option. Or, watch your students while they attend other classes expressly to find those brief moments where you can spot the student doing well or in a short transitional behavior that you can identify as a success.

## Creative Recognition: No-Fail Directives

This is a type of creative recognition that will work with the most challenging student—a child who seems bent on doing nothing in accordance with your requests. No-fail directives can be fun, but you have to be sincere to make them work.

Just glance at the student and give him a directive *while he is in the act.* For example: say "Get your desk cleared" to a student who is already doing so. Then, praise his forethought, his amazing anticipation, his quick estimation of what needed to happen, and his great example to others.

> ## Existence = Success
> Link the child's very existence to something great and wonderful.
> "Class wouldn't be as vital without you."
> "Your presence adds a needed calmness to the class."
> "I like seeing how the other students smile when you enter the room."
> "Hey—there you are! Great to have your opinion in the room."

## Putting it All Together

All four of these techniques are intended to help you look deeper into the intentions and motivations of students who seem to present problems. Most of the world's great inventions sprang from problems that inspired someone to think "outside the box" to solve them. When confronted with a difficult student or classroom, we can wonder where the buried treasure lies in wait for the relentless seeker of the positive!

It takes about two seconds to hand a student a positive recognition. Theoretically, it would be possible to do 100 recognitions in five minutes but this is by no means realistic or even desired under our approach. **Think about how much time you already spend settling disruptions, writing a detention, or getting students focused. And add to that the time you may already be spending (perhaps five minutes an hour) making statements of simple praise like "thank you" and "good job." By spending five minutes per hour on the more powerful positives we are suggesting, you will likely save much more time—and be less drained, with a room full of happy students.** Imagine how transformative this would be for every child. We've seen firsthand how classrooms have blossomed under showers of praise from teachers.

All these techniques build on one another and are designed to be used in a fluid way and in combination. You can successfully use them one at a time, but you'll build a more effortless and convincing vocabulary of praises as you learn to mix and match the four kinds of recognition.

The simplicity and brevity of this approach are the key to its effectiveness. It cuts to the heart of information that's needed to motivate a challenging child. If your praises or requests get too vague or long-winded, you may end up sending the wrong message. Keep working to make what the student can value in his or her self abundantly clear.

## Stand Up and Praise—Loud and Clear, Front and Center

Mr. P had a class of about 28 students who were very talkative, impulsive, and distractible. For several weeks, he had been constantly handing out "Thank You" notes with beautiful reflections of inner wealth, and he was doing his best to be strict. Some co-workers were using "Chill" cards to signal that a time-out was being given, and Mr. P was rapidly traversing the room with those as well. Yet the class was not getting much better.

Mr. P tended to walk around the room during class, and it turned out that students would only shape up when he was physically near them. As he moved away, they would resume poor behavior. He used a fairly quiet voice when issuing his recognitions and thus was not a major source of energy that dominated the room. More succinctly: he wasn't speaking loudly enough. As a result, the economy of inner wealth and strictness was only occurring in a small perimeter around him as he walked the room. It was not THE economy. Nor was Mr. P able to see the whole room, so he could not respond easily and quickly to the variety of successes and rule-breaking going on.

In Ms. K's room, things were difficult, too. Like Mr. P, she would walk the room and have little conversations with students, kneeling down beside them. It was hard to see and hear her unless you were right near her. Students would be looking around the room trying to find her, but she was often crouching down and essentially hidden. Again, the teacher was not present to the whole room— only to a small cluster of students at a time—and she was not creating a clear economy of abundant recognitions. In fact, students had to create quite a commotion to even be observed. Ms. K felt like she was always chasing a new fire.

Here's an analogy to what's transpiring in these classrooms. I am driving along and see that a state trooper is stopped with someone else at the side of the road. If I zoom by at 90 mph, she is in a poor position to enforce rules, and if I'm obeying the rules, she's not in a position to praise me. She is tied up in another problem and her eyes are off the whole flow on the interstate. It would take a loud noise or disturbance to shift her attention. Don't think for a second that students can't assess this and provide the level of disturbance needed to get the desired engagement.

The solution for both teachers was to get up front and LOUDLY broadcast inner wealth as well as time-outs. When this shift was made, students could be instantly energized with a recognition or put in time-out from across the room. There was no longer a need for Mr. P to travel around with "chill" cards or "thank you" notes, and both teachers now had the attention of all students. By being LOUD, both teachers were able to make plenty of energy available, advertising that they were rapidly responsive to success as well as broken rules.

It may seem odd that we are recommending LOUD time-outs. Isn't that giving the problem a lot of attention? If you pour a lot of energy into it, yes. We're recommending that you speak loudly in a matter-of-fact way. It is your intention to have all students learn from the recognition or the time-out you bestow on any one. Again, the rules are just the rules and you have no emotional investment in them. All you are doing is fearlessly enforcing at a level at which everyone in the room can be aware.

Both teachers were busy celebrating student success and enforcing rules, but on too small a scale. Once they got up front and kept their eyes on the whole class, and boldly squeezed everyone into the economy of the approach as an unavoidable presence, the rooms improved. Another way of looking at this is to say the teacher let every student know they could rapidly have relationship with the teacher from anywhere in the room—not just in a four-foot circle around the teacher. The students then didn't have to try as hard to engage the teacher. The quiet success of the student would now be sufficient to readily capture the teacher's relationship.

It is very effective to broadcast praise across the room rather than having it be a semi-private or individual encounter between you and a student. (The same goes for consequences; more on that in Chapter Five.) Everyone will know what you're being captured by; everyone will see that positive recognition from you is available to them as well.

When working with teachers, we usually advise them to stay at the front of the classroom when dealing with a difficult group. Once the teacher drifts to the back of the room, the high relationship rollers toss the dice and hope they'll get away with some infraction without the teacher seeing it. The teacher often misses this from the back of the room. When students are working fairly quietly and independently, teachers can take more license to wander around and give more one-on-one recognitions. But if the group decompensates, get up to the front, praise, and enforce rules.

Some day soon, both of these teachers will be able to wander about the room, spend more independent time with individual students, leave the room, have long periods of quiet, and not need to be so intense. Their classrooms, like yours, will be a calm oasis for students that you and they will treasure.

# Chapter Four

## *Building Inner Wealth*

ONCE WE GET STUDENTS TO BEHAVE, it's human nature for us to say to ourselves, *"Finally!* That's the way she should have acted in the first place!"

The natural tendency is to then move straight to the most important business: academic progress. Some teachers realize that, once they do get all their students to behave, they have perhaps 10 minutes before the next conflagration. They leap into the lesson, teaching at 290 miles per hour to get as much into students' heads as possible before the amazing balancing act falls apart.

After all, teachers have lesson plans and curricula that must be covered by certain timeframes. If not, they're behind. They have not done their job. Standardized test scores will be lower and the school or teacher will be labeled a failure. Funding could be lost, as could the teacher's job. This is a high-pressure situation for everyone involved.

An approach that pushes the lesson also is not conducive to the creation of inner wealth, which we maintain is at the root of any successful attempt to educate a child. In the Nurtured Heart Approach, the real goal is imbuing the skills it takes to learn—*above the learning itself.* When we praise those skills, we enhance the child's inner wealth in ways that encourage her *to learn* to learn and to *love learning.*

If you are trying to fill a cup with a lid on it, you're going to have a big mess to mop up. By creating inner wealth, confidence, and self-esteem in the classroom, we take off the lid, allowing all that crisp, clear, refreshing knowledge to flow more freely into the vessel—the child. We're creating fishermen, not just handing someone a fish. The desire for knowledge becomes a core force field that makes the job of imparting knowledge delightful because the student is there with you every step of the way.

## First, A Few Common (Great) Questions

Before presenting more about what inner wealth is and how to create it, we want to address a few concerns that tend to come up in workshops and meetings with school personnel as they begin to digest the thrust of this approach. These are great inquiries, and the answers teachers receive can make or break their willingness to try the approach.

**Q:** *Is this another soft, sweet, enabling, overlooking, grandma's-love kind of approach?*

**A:** When teachers first hear that the approach is about the "nurtured heart," some are turned off. They think it's too soft and sweet to give them the answers they need for the tough discipline problems they face. Tom Grove has turned most such doubters into big advocates, but sometimes it took months of effort to get them to even try a training. So, the short answer to this question is most definitely *no*—it **is not enabling or soft or fuzzy.** It is firm and strict—and the positives are indeed nurturing, but they're also another way of playing hardball. And you can't play hardball with limits until you play hardball with success.

**Q:** *Why should I praise children for just doing what they ought to be doing in the first place?*

**A:** For starters, let's keep in mind that some students have been so far off the map that simply doing what they should amounts to a huge success! Even those of us who don't have issues can be considered successful when doing what we ought to do, or when we ask for the help we need to do those things.

We've all heard the jokes about men who refuse to ask for directions and the travails that ensue for everyone in the car with them. What if we were to shower that driver with appreciation when he finally gave in and pulled into a gas station to get directions (instead of snapping, "If you'd DONE this a hundred MILES ago, we'd BE there already!!")? If we were genuine and specific about that recognition, the next family vacation might not involve quite so much navigational guesswork.

There are probably 80 gazillion self-help books currently on the shelves that all, in some way or another, tell us what we really should already know. It's helpful to remember this when we get frustrated over students not seeming to know the most basic guidelines for behaving or learning.

This is not to minimize the courage it takes to be totally lost and ask for help. Many of us are conditioned to believe that asking for help is an admission that we aren't cutting it somehow—that we aren't smart enough or good enough. The Nurtured Heart Approach creates an environment of positivity and trust where this risk can be more easily taken. Students learn to ask for help in ways that enable you to help them more effectively.

When we use the Nurtured Heart Approach, we are actually reflecting children's *character—who they are in relation to their actions.* We notice what they do as a manifestation of their character—an effect caused by their basic and essential goodness. You describe their character as they perform common, expected tasks; when they exhibit exemplary behaviors; when they don't engage in negative behaviors; when they make good choices; when they apply learning skills; or when they react to or treat other people in respectful or otherwise positive ways. These comments serve to give their life meaning and hope, to make them feel useful, and to help them feel they have a place in the bigger picture—that they are valuable and valued.

Think of it as updated software that we download—a new set of programs that serve to further tune children's ever-evolving inner guidance system. In the child's mind and soul, someone else's comments and perceptions of her cause her to feel wiser and more attuned. That experience becomes the updated version of who she is. The positive repercussions will ripple out into how she now negotiates the world.

If you don't think it makes sense to praise behaviors that students should automatically engage in, you will be able to find something else to praise that reflects their character or spirit. We encourage teachers to praise both the commonplace and the extraordinary.

Unfortunately, some students just don't adhere to the standards of decent, respectful behavior; they don't do what they should. With those students, we have to start someplace. As we work to minimize the relationship and energy given to problems, we begin positively energizing even their smallest steps toward what they should do in the first place. In other circumstances, we may want to pursue the positive by ignoring the student when he isn't doing the expected while recognizing those students who are, which may help redirect the problematic student. If we accomplish this, we can then give a positive reflection to that student for redirecting himself. Either way, the student learns what will energize relationship for him.

Bottom line: there are students who just *do not know* what is expected, and there are also students who make a conscious or subconscious choice *not to do* what they know is expected. Either way, our approach works. They get detailed information about what's expected, and they also see that meeting those expectations will yield a wonderful sense of connection to others.

Q: *What about the student who just wants out of class no matter what—the one who can't do the work and just wants to hang out with someone at in-school suspension?*

A: This common question has several components that need to be addressed individually. First, the obvious: if the student can't do the work, she needs help so that she can. Avoiding the problem will not help anyone. Some students have put two and two together, realizing that by not doing their work—as an act of negativity or rebellion rather than because of any inability to do it—they receive quite a bit of quality time, energy and relationship. Consider this before assuming that the student "can't" do the work.

Secondly, you'll need to address the amount of relationship available in your school's in-school suspension program. Whatever is compelling to the student at in-school suspension, your classroom needs to offer something more compelling. In-school suspension, if it has to happen, should feel like a time-out to the student, not a holiday.

What really works against a student wanting to escape is a classroom that has a wonderful time-in. When a student is given concrete evidence that he belongs and is competent, valued, and abundantly and unshakably enjoyed, *he will want to be there.* This is the social curriculum—the time-in—in action. The child finds that he is important and successful as a person, aside from his ability to fulfill the academic curriculum. New academic abilities typically blossom as well.

Q: *Won't all this positive recognition take up my teaching time?*

A: Actually, it will probably increase your teaching time significantly. Spending five minutes on the social curriculum will *accelerate* your academic curriculum as students show increasingly wonderful social interaction with you and with their peers. A positive learning environment prevails; their "learning to learn" skills and their dedication to learning flourish. (More on this later in this chapter.)

Q: *What if my aide or co-teacher doesn't use this approach?*

A: It is becoming common practice in some states to pair up a new teacher with a more experienced co-teacher or aide. While this can offer invaluable support and has been found to help reduce the attrition of new teachers, problems can arise when one teacher wishes to use the Nurtured Heart Approach and the other does not. Negativity from someone else can really undermine your efforts to create a positive atmosphere in the classroom.

Many in the world of education believe that having extra adult help in a classroom is automatically highly desirable without necessarily questioning the nature of the help. It is crucial that all the adults in a given room are on the same page. With today's growing number of broken families, too many children are already feeling the effects of mixed signals or even negativity in their home environments due to conflicting styles of child-raising. It would be unfortunate to exacerbate this situation by not presenting a unified stance in the classroom.

It's great to have the extra help if all are working in concert; but ultimately, it can be much easier for one teacher by herself to get great changes to happen. This is particularly true if others who work in the classroom are unwilling to practice the Nurtured Heart Approach.

If you are faced with a non-complying co-worker, we urge you to plow ahead with the approach in your classroom, and use the Nurtured Heart Approach to build the inner wealth of your co-worker, too. Or attempt to get the co-worker to try out the Nurtured Heart Approach for two to three weeks and see what the effects are; this has won some non-believers over entirely.

As a last resort, where the kind of agreement described above seems impossible, be prolific at implementing the approach to the point where the other teacher or aide has little chance to enter into negative relationship with students. In effect, one teacher prevents the other from spending energy on problems and escalating the students. Our experience shows that the results of the Nurtured Heart Approach are so amazing as to eventually win over the doubters.

Remember that few teachers—or any adults, for that matter—have ever been in an environment of sustained positives and deep character affirmation such as the one found in a Nurtured Heart classroom. You, with your students, will be going into uncharted territory where there is no fussing, shaming, arguing, threatening, or failure. There will only be success, or "resets" that quickly end before success continues.

**Q: *Won't all that praise get old and lose its impact and meaning?***

**A:** The evidence from Tolson Elementary School and many others clearly indicates "no." Students keep thriving and developing with this approach as they mature and encounter new life issues. The sustained, positive environment provided with the Nurtured Heart Approach is the foundation on which students can rely as they develop and face new challenges.

Praise that is vague and lacks evidence *does* get tiresome—and, eventually, downright annoying. Much of the learning curve of the Nurtured Heart Approach, for both teachers and parents, involves *mastering the art of specific and effective articulation of appreciation and acknowledgment.* "Oh, that's interesting" doesn't tell me you really like my new shirt or what I'm writing about. "I love you" without congruent actions of love becomes painful. Even evidence-based compliments without sincerity ring as dull and empty, or even sarcastic. This is like someone saying they're sorry for not showing up as promised when their tone says they couldn't care less. *If you use praise as a tool for control without sincerity and honesty to back it up, it doesn't contain the authenticity that gives your words their ultimate meaningfulness and impact. Students will quickly detect that you are not truly interested in their inner wealth, and the approach will lose its influence.*

Insincere praise and recognitions can end up backfiring as the child's resentment builds. She knows she's being fed a line and that you're trying to control her. That's why we use specific, evidence-based recognitions and praise in the Nurtured Heart Approach. When it's done right, this kind of acknowledgment stays as fresh as the moment in which each example of acknowledgment occurs. They nurture the heart of the recipient.

## Inner Wealth Is Its Own Curriculum

The rule we are about to share with you has already been mentioned in this book. We mention it again here because it's a major stumbling block when most teachers start up the steep slope of the learning curve of this approach. Once a teacher learning the Nurtured Heart Approach catches on to this point and demonstrates that he understands it by following it time after time, Tom Grove can sometimes be seen in the back of the room actually jumping for joy. It is so simple, yet so hard, for teachers to follow this rule. It's hard for anyone, really. The rule is:

**When you get good behavior from the class, PRAISE INNER WEALTH! Do not jump into teaching.**

This is the most important thing to remember when trying to build inner wealth in your students. Be a ruthless opportunist. Keep this close to your heart as you continue through this chapter and work to apply its concepts in your classroom.

Teachers, as with most adults, tend to be very limited in the particular vocabulary necessary for talking in varyious robust and inspiring ways about the skills and qualities they wish to recognize, enhance and deepen in their students. Probably 99 percent of the teachers we work with start out struggling to find the right words. Without the vocabulary, recognition isn't going to roll off your tongue.

We would like to help you get accustomed to firing off positives without a lot of effort. That vocabulary comes from a deep understanding of the character, coping, learning and social skills that fit into this remarkable social curriculum.

Aside from recognizing good behavioral choices and appropriate values, as described in previous chapters, we can help students achieve academically **by recognizing behaviors, attitudes, and attributes that make them ready and receptive to learning.** For example:

| | |
|---|---|
| Readiness | Inducting |
| Attentiveness | Deducting |
| Cooperation | Intuitiveness |
| Patience | Listening |
| Reflectiveness | Participating |
| Problem-solving | Prepared |
| Wondering | Organized |
| Guessing | Alert |
| Asking | Inquisitive |
| Comparing | Collaborative |
| Self-control | Receptive |
| Remembering | Present |

Basically the list could include anything else it takes to become an angler for knowledge.

Once the children in your classroom see that your energy will flow their way when they are open to and striving for learning, your days of high G-force teaching will be largely over.

When the class begins to behave, recognize them with specifics for showing what it takes to learn. Don't demonstrate to students that you value the lesson over them by leaping into the lesson as soon as they're quiet and seem attentive. *As soon as you do that, they'll see your new fabulously positive approach as a manipulation, and the fireworks will begin anew.*

The more you give positive, energized relationship to students simply for being receptive and present in your classroom, the sooner they will be ready to learn and the better they will demonstrate ability to learn. They will know you value and enjoy them above any academic exercise or lesson.

The curriculum of teaching students that they are good and valuable people is the most lasting lesson a teacher can ever teach. The time you put into this will improve your classroom's academic performance. But, ironically, to enjoy the **fullest expression** of your students' academic mastery and achievement, you have to go after the prize of inner wealth, not the prize of better grades or test scores.

*Not everyone can be brilliant, but they can be wonderful participants, valued, and enjoyed—and feel great about themselves.*

As a teacher, as an administrator, as a parent, view children as though they are continually making decisions to be well-behaved, kind, and productive. We all do this as adults, all the time: we decide to be kind when we are really tempted to blow a gasket and say something mean; we try a task again even though we are frustrated; we sit through a meeting we think is a waste of time yet we're polite, attentive, and make a contribution. In so many ways, we choose to do well, every day. We're being good on purpose! Minute by minute! *So are your students.* Let them know that you recognize this by praising their choices.

Study the many facets of inner wealth described in this chapter. Begin to search for others. Since it can be challenging to do this while teaching, spend time outside your teaching time simply observing. Go to other classrooms and look for what's going right, even when things seem to be going wrong in many ways. For a real challenge, try the lunchroom!

- **Look for tiny moments of compliance, effort, kindness, and self-control. Recognize your own success in seeing these positive attributes and traits.**
- **Try breaking tasks like finding the right page in a textbook, raising a hand, or working with a group into the many positive factors required to do those tasks.**

Here's an example of how this works in the classroom.[6] Mr. Y made special efforts to praise his students' willingness to both answer and ask questions in his

---

6. All of the examples given in this book are real, drawn from the experiences of the authors in classrooms with teachers learning the model, or from what they were told by teachers about their experiences.

science class. It did not matter how off-the-mark the answer or question was; just the act of asking or answering was praised as brave, courageous, or helpful to others trying to understand. It probably comes as no surprise that, in this classroom, both asking and answering greatly increased. The lessons became richer. Children who did not have a clue began to try to openly grasp the lesson, because doing so had become safe and rewarding. Soon it became rare that anyone laughed at a question or answer. During the second nine weeks, 11 of the 22 students improved their grades. Only four students dropped a grade—and then only from a straight letter to a minus or from a plus to a straight letter.

In Shamu terms, this is equivalent to rewarding Shamu for aiming toward the rope, being in the right area, looking at the rope, swimming at the right speed—any other factor that might lead Shamu to actually swim over the rope. Or, put another way: *if you want Shamu to swim over the rope and he almost never does, put the rope everywhere!*

## What Is Inner Wealth?

Inner wealth is whatever it takes to cope, be happy, and grow within ourselves and with other people. It is multifaceted and deeply connected to our feeling that we are significantly and meaningfully part of humanity just by virtue of being alive.

So what does it take to cope, be happy in our spirit, and thrive? There are many answers and hundreds of books about what it takes. We humbly offer our two cents' worth on this topic. *(Please see pages 68–69).*

There are, undoubtedly, many other factors that constitute inner wealth. That is one of the beautiful aspects of this approach. There is always much to recognize and celebrate; always something going well, even when other things aren't picture perfect. Take just a few factors we have listed and start to observe them in yourself and others. As you work on your students' inner wealth, experiment with building your own inner wealth. Opportunistically note and enjoy your own efforts and successes. Experiment with new and expanded ways of varying your inner wealth vocabulary. Think about variations on the theme of appreciation and recognition.

## Building Inner Wealth

To build inner wealth is to find a myriad number of ways to recognize, describe, and celebrate a student's heart, spirit, and character. We fearlessly, relentlessly pursue evidence with which to validate qualities of inner wealth.

Building inner wealth in our students requires that we find this evidence in what students do; in what they *don't* do; and in their intentions, hopes, successes, and even failures. It requires that we strive to have a laser-like focus on steps toward success in our students and that we remain strict even while freely offering forgiveness and redemption. To build students' inner wealth, we must be able to enact a consequence *even while having complete faith in the student's ability to do better*—and then quickly find reason to justify that faith in the student. This creates tremendous hope within the student, even the most pessimistic student—especially as we unfold our appreciation in the way they are treated.

We can't cultivate inner wealth with pep talks. Whereas pep talks are attempts to encourage desired qualities, the Nurtured Heart Approach actually embeds these qualities into the fabric of the student's actual experience. By verbally cherishing those qualities as they occur in real time, we help the child's inner experience become congruent with actual possession of that quality. The child doesn't have to hope and pray that he'll have that quality someday if he just tries hard enough; he sees that today, right now, he embodies it—it's already inside him. This way, he has ownership and control.

We are creating success as the only option. It will transform the portfolio of what and who students perceive they are, and what they think they will be.

## Encourage Students to Think in Ways That Increase Their Inner Wealth

When students have questions, you can divert that energy into the creation of inner wealth by asking them what they could do to find their own answers. Ask students what they are doing really well in this moment, or why they are getting positive recognitions. Ask the entire class to assess their own noise level or any other aspect of the classroom's behavior that you consider a sign of success. Questions such as these give students an opportunity to recognize their own correctness, awareness, self-monitoring, etc. You are teaching them to trust their own judgment rather than just listen to yours.

Again, we're creating fishermen instead of tossing fish. This creates self-monitoring feedback systems within students that give rise to more and more inner wealth and more opportunities for praise and recognition.

In our experience with youth, we have often been amazed at the major lack of relationship language students tend to have. They know how to recognize success at the "good job" or "thank you" level—of course, because that is how *they* have been recognized. Most believe that they can only be a great person when they have done something spectacular. Many students have lives of quiet despair and have given up on the prospects of anything going that well. The Nurtured Heart Approach teaches them new and creative language and feedback systems to help them know, recognize, and verbally express "great person."

Having students think about what's going on right now, about what things might mean, about what they are doing, and about ways to find their own answers and solutions to problems promotes all sorts of inner wealth. We are helping students cultivate confidence, patience, calmness, self-awareness, awareness of others, independence, helpfulness, a richer vocabulary, creative thinking, differentiation, ego development, and the ability to compare and contrast. So much more then for you, as their teacher, to appreciate!

# Inner Wealth is:

The ability to endure and persevere

Character marked by self-control, optimism, and kindness

Patience

Hope

Trust in ourselves

The ability to make and keep agreements

The ability to solve problems

The ability to forgive

The ability to listen well and value what others have to say

Being able to fully feel without fear of feelings

Being able to be in the moment

Being able to plan ahead

Feeling healthy power and equality

Having love, grace and compassion for others—
and for ourselves

Being organized enough to finish things

Having courage to change

Being able to choose long-term spiritual joy over short-term,
sensation-based excitement

Being creative, reflective, expressive

Knowing you are lovable

Being truthful

Taking responsibility for what we do or do not do

Being able to see the intentions of others

Being responsive and connected to what a situation calls for

Thinking that people have a good reason for what they do

Knowing the most precious and enduring things are invisible

Being willing to befriend others

Having the skills to express yourself

Sensing the hopes and dreams of others

Being able to experience wonder and awe

Having the ability to find divine love in mundane or
unfortunate events

Making the world a softer place

Giving support and kindness to others

Choosing to see the beauty in the world

Being thankful and grateful

Showing integrity and making honorable choices

Making intelligent decisions

Using excellent judgment

*Add your own aspects of inner wealth below if you like:*

_____

_____

_____

_____

_____

_____

## "Machine Gun-Rate" Praise

Kids need to see and feel the possibility of their greatness. So many of our children have no prior experience of this. Experiencing one's inner strength makes it possible to call it up when you really need it.

Once you feel you can easily see streams of inner wealth flowing from students, begin studying the language and phrases suggested later in this chapter in the section "Good Job." It may be hard to break the habit of tossing out "good job" and "thank you" in response to good choices made by your students. Congratulate yourself each and every time you make more of an impact with a more elaborate statement of appreciation. Make some cue cards, or pick three phrases and wear them out. Then, pick three more and wear them out. Get your storehouse of phrases loaded up to the rafters.

As you become more adept, experiment with tossing those praises out at higher and higher rates until you've reached what Tom Grove has dubbed "machine gun-rate." Teachers who have developed this skill are able to maximize the benefits of the Nurtured Heart Approach in their classrooms and beyond. *They become absolutely fearless in applying the approach.*

In rooms where things are going well and there are just a few difficult students, do your best to *match or exceed* the rate and intensity of relationship displayed by the students. Machine gun-rate praise enables you to do this with ease. We have watched several great classrooms unravel because the rate of praise was too low.

Mrs. J's classroom was running fairly smoothly after a week of machine gun-rate praising from Mrs. J and the aide. She was covering more lessons, but her praise rate was falling too rapidly to sustain the progress she'd made. As she praised, more and more students began to call out: "What about me, Mrs. J?" "I've been good too, Mrs. J!" "Tell me *I've* been working hard, too!" **Behaved students are not necessarily transformed students—and the goal is transformation, not good behavior.** Once you know your students have been transformed—and believe us, you'll know when that has occurred—your rate of praise can decline and your students can sustain themselves for substantially longer periods.

Difficult children are often highly sensitive people who can easily experience withdrawal from positive relationship. Many are starving for positive recognition, and the rate that might sustain you or others you know may fall far short for them.

Use your creativity. Invent your own dazzling phrases to celebrate students' inner wealth!

## Holding Up the Mirror

We refer to one main method of building up inner wealth as "holding up a mirror." We are reflecting to the student who she is as a person. This is done in such a way that the student gets all the credit for her success and the valued qualities she manifests. Holding up the mirror is not about reflecting how student behavior is pleasing to us, but *reflecting the student as a person so she can be pleased with herself*. Consider this example of how important it is to reflect the heart, spirit, and character of students to them:

Ms. H has seven classes that totally change every nine weeks. She uses a questionnaire to rapidly get to know students. One question asks, "What is unique about you as a person?" A student called her over and said that this question confused him. He asked what it meant. She replied, "I want to know something special about who you are."

"I could write down that I have ADHD," the student said.

"Yes, but that is something you have, not who you are," Ms. H replied, but the student looked bewildered. "I want to know things like...how you are brave, generous, creative, thoughtful, things like that."

Everyone "has" something. Maybe it's diabetes, maybe a deformity, maybe great beauty, or a great talent. What a person *has* is not who a person *is*. Inner wealth is *who you are*. Like the student above, many people do not know or do not have the language to describe and reflect on who they are. Many of us have never been fully introduced to how many wonderful qualities we possess. Thus, the importance of holding up the mirror and giving clear reflections for students.

Back to Ms. H. One day, she was welcoming a new class. As they entered, she began to double-dip them in reflections of inner wealth—before even asking them their names:

"Oh, I see you are very observant and correctly deduced your correct seat!"

"WOW, you are so patient and considerate by waiting for me to call on you!"

"I notice you know how to really pay attention and have kept eye contact with me!"

On and on she went, reflecting and injecting inner wealth and success into the center of her new students' life force. There was joy to spare and zero problems among the entire class.

Just after that class left, a new group of students came in. She began asking names and saying things like:

"Thank you for raising your hand."

"I like how you are sitting very appropriately."

"I appreciate the way you are being patient."

Soon, she needed to administer a couple of time-outs. Despite thanking students for completing the time-outs and despite handing out thank-you notes to students for sitting quietly, working, and recovering after a time-out, another time-out was needed.

In comparing the two class periods, it becomes clear that the first class got reflections of a *richer quality* than the second class. In the first class, the reflections were loaded with inner wealth, inspiring students to be totally excited about themselves. In the second class, the reflections were primarily about good behavior that pleased Ms. H.

A student may or may not glean some good feelings from pleasing a teacher or feel valued because they please someone. Severely dependent people know how to please people but rarely accumulate inner wealth of their own. In Ms. H's second class, the messages added up to "I'm attending to you because you know how to behave, and that makes me happy." In the first class, the messages very clearly reflected back the students' individual greatness.

**The building of inner wealth has nothing to do with students pleasing us or making us happy.** It has everything to do with us providing students with evidence about themselves so they can be pleased and thrilled with what they see in that mirror we're holding up. This is not the magic mirror from Disney movies that actually talks about what it reflects; it is a plain old mirror, wiped sparkling clean, that reflects inner wealth back on the student.

We can share in that joy of discovery and awareness, but students do not need to strive for or worry about us liking them. We reflect how wonderful and likeable they are because we like them already! They are already wonderful to us! We need only to freely, generously *reflect* their success. We are striving to show them that we are already grateful! We show this by validating that they are ALREADY successful, ALREADY worthy of our joy, and ALREADY deeply appreciated. The mirror reflects all the glorious light back upon the students and convinces them that it is indeed their being that we are so thrilled about.

More examples:

Ms. H realized from the mounting number of time-outs that time-in needed to be highly enriched. She began to celebrate and reflect all the joy and light back upon the students. Time-outs became unnecessary; everyone began to wait for their next moment of deep and powerful connection with reflections of who they are.

Mr. Y asked Marleena what she had done over the weekend. Marleena said she learned to play golf. Mr. Y asked her how she liked it, how she did, and if she was going to try again. This is typical chit-chat, which many people would see as relationship building, connecting, or perhaps signaling progress in an otherwise discordant relationship. It could be all that and more. It presents a beautiful opportunity to hold up a mirror and reflect inner wealth:

"Marleena, it's very ambitious of you to try golf."

"Marleena, you really know how to get out there and enjoy life."

"I imagine your determination at basketball will take you to success in golf as well."

Chit-chat pales in comparison to the relationship that occurs when someone sees treasure in us—and wants us to have every penny of it.

This is very important. Holding up a mirror and reflecting wonderful qualities that students already possess asks nothing of them. They are not being required to please us. They are not made to feel that they owe us something. It is all theirs in the first place and we are just shining it back upon them. They do not have to earn our admiration because we admire them in the first place. They do not have to earn their significance because we see them as significant in the first place.

When you do this, you may get some interesting reactions. Students may say "You don't really know me," or "That's not who I really am." Do not give a pep talk or argue. Just say something like "Well, to me that was truly [insert your reflection]," and move on. Reflect other positives to them so they don't think you are trying to prove a point just so that you can "be right" about them.

## Bye-Bye, Bullying; Hello, Inner Wealth

National surveys find that about 30 percent of teens are involved in bullying, either as a target, a bully, or both. In one 2001 survey of students in sixth through tenth grades, 13 percent reported bullying others; 11 percent reported being targets of bullies; and six percent said they both bullied and were bullied.[7] Students who are tormented by bullies report being close to suicide as a result. Violence in schools foments more violence, as evidenced by tragic school shootings where students who had been bullied for years decided that a violent rampage was the best way out. A lot of money is being funneled into research efforts and school interventions to stop bullying.

Tolson Elementary School has had *zero bullying* since 1999 when the Nurtured Heart Approach was implemented school-wide. When kids feel great about themselves, they don't want to be hurtful to others. They become appreciative and helpful toward others and want to support one another. Inner wealth takes the wind out of the sails of bullying. Everyone benefits.

When inner wealth is present and ever-expanding, children's valuation of themselves is enhanced. They take better care of themselves, developing improved eating and exercise habits. They *want* to do their homework and do it well; they want to get to school on time and get to know their teachers. Parents and teachers find that they no longer have to micromanage children. The child can steer on his or her own. It is reasonable to expect that results such as those achieved at Tolson, if expanded across school districts, would reduce drug use, smoking, and teen pregnancy.

Howie Glasser has seen in his own teenage daughter that inner wealth helps her avoid negative peer pressures: she sees when a friend is making poor choices, and instead of getting sucked into that herself, chooses instead to move out of that friend's circle. True to her dad's approach, she doesn't give her energy to her friend's negativity.

---

7. Nansel, T.R., Overpeck, M., Pilla, R.S., Ruan, W.J., Simons-Morton, B., and Scheidt, P. (2001). Bullying behaviors among U.S. youth: Prevalence and association with psychosocial adjustment. *Journal of the American Medical Association*, 285(16), 2094-2100.

When his daughter was in seventh grade, Howie spent some time sitting in on her classes to get to know her teachers. He observed very clearly that students with stronger inner wealth stayed totally focused on the lesson even when the teacher turned his back, while others would explode into play mode or social mode. He saw that the kids who stayed focused were the kids who felt great about themselves. They wanted to learn—what a concept! School isn't boring when you care about yourself and about how much you can learn!

## More Real-Life Examples of Teachers Building Inner Wealth in the Classroom

Mr. Y had just handed Quin a detention slip for disrupting the class. Quin said nothing, reached out and put it in his notebook. Mr. Y said, "Quin, you accepted this detention without any hesitation or problem. You are a person of integrity and honor for acknowledging what you did and accepting the consequence. That is something to be proud of."

Long after that detention is over and done with, Mr. Y's celebration of Quin's inner wealth will reverberate—not only in Quin, but also in the other students who heard it. Mr. Y was fearlessly living in the moment, relentlessly focusing on the positive as it manifested itself, and holding positives up for celebration and appreciation. He demonstrated to his students that talking out and fussing in class is nothing compared to integrity, honor, and pride.

A few weeks later Quin was talking out and rapidly earned a trip to the office under the rules of the school at the time. As Mr. Y delivered the pass for the office, Quin said, "I think I can do better tomorrow, Mr. Y," and walked out calmly and quietly. As he left, Mr. Y said, "I look forward to seeing you in class tomorrow."

The next day, Quin was entirely successful. Mr. Y recognized and celebrated this with numerous comments. *More importantly, Quin had become more powerful than his problem.* He showed integrity and behaved honorably. Everyone knew Quin was trying. A few days later, after a totally successful class, the other students spontaneously applauded Quin for his success that day. Accomplishments like these—on the part of both the teacher and the student—give us goose bumps. We hope it does the same for you.

Alex had a history of fighting and talked about how important it was to be a good fighter in his neighborhood. One day, a student tried to taunt Alex, and he just sat there. Before anything else could happen, Mr. Y said, "Alex, that is great self-control. That is being a strong man. You're doing one of the hardest things in the world right now."

Self-control is the cornerstone of maturity, leadership, and success. It keeps relationships going forward. It helps us be a good friend and a good parent, worthy of respect. With self-control, we can avoid being exploited by others. To build this aspect of inner wealth in Alex, Mr. Y knew he should not focus on what Alex should or should not be doing about fighting. Instead, he focused on all the behaviors and qualities Alex is showing in the moment that make him more powerful than the problem. He found evidence that showed Alex, in a highly personal and immediate way, that a tremendously powerful person is one who can solve problems without fighting—not one who strives to be a good fighter.

## Recognizing and Celebrating Inner Wealth

As they begin this approach, many people find it hard to break the habit of saying "good job!" To truly build inner wealth in all kinds of students, you must find a myriad of ways to convey *wonderful person! important person! valuable person! successful person!*

What follows are some illustrations that may seem silly on the surface, but we believe they will increase your recognition of inner wealth and your ability to dispense effective and meaningful praises that will further enhance inner wealth.

### *The Pencil Sharpener and the Meatloaf: Two Instructive Tales*

Let's take two very ordinary tasks and break them down into many elements or steps. First: a student sharpening a pencil before class.

First of all, he has to remember that he needs a pencil. He has to keep track of it and be aware of its dull condition—or, perhaps, he has the discipline to remember to sharpen before class no matter what shape the pencil is in. He has to keep track of time to get his pencil sharpened before class period begins. Maybe he doesn't remember to sharpen at first, but he's aware of what others are doing and takes a cue from them. If there's a line, he needs to be able to take turns. He must gauge how long the pencil needs to be in the sharpener to get it just right and not grind it down too far or make the point too delicate. He needs to get to the sharpener and back without incident or commotion, and before going over there in the first place he has to make sure it is the pencil he really wants to use.

Such a multitude of acts might result from good planning, forethought, a good memory, being considerate of others, remembering the rules, paying attention to time, keeping track of important things, choosing to be a ready learner, being able to choose what is important, and so on. See how many ways a simple task like sharpening a pencil can be broken down? Each of those details could be used as an opportunity to promote inner wealth!

*The next time you think you couldn't possibly find a way to praise a student in your classroom—the one who just can't seem to get anything right—remember the pencil sharpener. Break down his actions into these same kinds of tiny choices and decisions, and you'll find plenty to celebrate!*

Another example Tom Grove likes to use is making a meatloaf. It starts with finding a recipe. For that, you need to read well or be a great listener. Then you have to figure out what you have on hand or need to buy. Somehow, you will need to list or remember what to buy at the store, and of course you'll need to find a way to get to the store. This may involve determining bus routes or driving safely there. You must avoid running over pedestrians around the store and park between the lines. Do you remember learning to drive and the challenge of parking before you had years of practice? In the store, you'll have to avoid breaking the rules or offending anyone in ways that could get you thrown out. This almost always involves extreme patience in the inevitable cart jams, and safely driving the cart. You have to find all the ingredients on your list and in the right amounts, too. If they are out of onions or ground beef, what will you do?

By the way, do you have a way to pay for this stuff? You also will require almost psychic talent or at least keen intuition to pick the checkout line that will not come to a screeching halt just before your turn. Think of the self-control (or is it empathy?) and patience needed when your intuition sends you to the wrong checkout line and time seems to stand still. You will need to make sure you are not being cheated and your coupons have not expired. Do you have enough gas to get home? Once safely home, there is the unloading.

Now you can start cooking. You have to know how to measure, cut the food and not your fingers, keep track of what you already mixed, and not spread microscopic time-bombs of bacteria everywhere. Did you forget to pick up the children at school? Did you forget to stop at the cleaners before closing time? Time to crack the eggs—remember learning to do that without getting bits of shell in the bowl? OK, time to pop that lovely meatloaf in the oven so dinner can be on the table at the right time. You must be skilled at using that appliance. Let's not forget that you had to be sure to choose a baking dish that would not melt in the oven. Will all the side dishes be done in concert with the meatloaf?

Finally, the meatloaf is successfully removed from the oven and ready for mass consumption. Now comes your big payoff, the reason you do what you do, the thing that makes it all worthwhile: "Tastes good! Good job."

The point is: all these facets reflect some quality of inner wealth. "Good job" doesn't come close to acknowledging the multitude of talents, choices, and self-control shown by the pencil sharpener or the meatloaf maker—or the student in your classroom who just does what's required every day. This is why we celebrate students who "just do what they're supposed to do" because, whatever they are doing, it represents talents and qualities they will need in many areas of life.

## Break It Down and Add It Up

Now, let's consider a few ways in which we can "dissect" students' choices, behaviors, and attitudes in ways that give you endless material for rapid-fire recognitions.

- When a student accepts a consequence with no fuss whatsoever, what positive qualities may be present in that student? A few likely possibilities: the student is honorable, has integrity, is responsible, is trustworthy, can handle strong emotions, has patience, is respectful of the class, and has great self-control.

- If you look at Suzy's house made of popsicle sticks, consider what she likely had in her that allowed such creation. She had to enter the classroom and go to the area where the art project was being done. She had to listen to the teacher's instructions about what the project would be for that day. Other praise-able behaviors and attributes might be: staying focused and concentrated for 10 to 20 minutes; coming up with her own creative design for her house; keeping the glue from getting all over herself or cleaning up a spill that did occur; not interfering with the work of others around her; handing a classmate materials when asked; and so on.

## "Create" Them in the Act

Another potent exercise is to take some video of your classroom and stop it at short intervals simply to find as many positive behaviors, positive choices and positive attitudes as you can. Do this with another teacher or friend for more opinions and ideas. You could also do this as a fun and illuminating exercise at a faculty meeting as staff are arriving. You will be amazed at how many positives are occurring minute by minute. These positives are opportunities to build inner wealth in the students, yourself and co-workers.

When students enter the room and sit at their desks, waiting for class to start, how many skills of their heart, mind, and spirit are at work? Many undesirable behaviors could be exhibited, so what is at work that prevents these behaviors from occurring?

In his book *The Power of Intention,* Dr. Wayne Dyer writes about research demonstrating the neurochemical changes that happen in a person who receives an act of kindness. When you are kind to someone by complimenting, acknowledging, or otherwise positively reinforcing them, the person's levels of the anti-depressant neurotransmitter serotonin rise. And here's the kicker: the serotonin levels of the *giver* of the act of kindness rise, too, as do the serotonin levels of any onlookers who observe this transaction of kindness! The research shows that this positive interaction also boosts the immune function of all involved parties. Talk about win-win! Or perhaps more appropriately: win-win-win-win-win-win-win!

## Flipping Problems: The Relentless Pursuit of the Positive

Teachers can often find wonderful successes manifesting in their students' behaviors from moment to moment. A student does something amazing, and the teacher reflects that moment in the mirror of inner wealth. It's a celebration of some positive action or the student's restraint from acting undesirably. This is the most basic level of recognition applied in the Nurtured Heart Approach. However, there is a deeper level of success to be found, which in turn produces a deeper and more powerful transformation. This level is reached through the *relentless pursuit of the positive*—that first leg of the three-legged table.

In Mr. T's science lab, there were teams of three students, each with a specific part of the project to fulfill. Alane complained that she was bored and had nothing to do because Nick was hogging all the materials and doing everything himself.

As a teacher, what would your initial reaction to this situation be? Would you admonish Nick for not sharing? Or would you admonish Alane for not taking the issue up with Nick directly? Maybe you'd just quietly take some of the materials from Nick and distribute them to the other two students in his group. *Any of these responses would, in the context of this approach, be leaks of negativity.* You might be solving the problem at hand, but you aren't instilling inner wealth or creating a rich, rewarding time-in.

A more positive approach might be to praise Alane for not yelling at her classmate; for not grabbing from Nick; or for asserting herself clearly, with a reasonable voice level. Let's take the praise a bit deeper and pursue the positive a little more relentlessly by looking further into Alane's complaint. It may spring from a deep desire to learn; to be part of a team; to be responsible for her own part of the assignment; to be brave and speak up when she feels that justice isn't being done; to excel in science; to be productive. Do you see how this is a deeper level of praise that says not only "great behavior" but "great, incredible, amazing, achieving, wonderful person"?

The latter is what actually happened in Mr. T's classroom. Once he had finished celebrating Alane's inner wealth and motivations, he asked her what she thought she herself could do to remedy the situation. Alane came up with two ideas that were viable and worthy of even more of the teacher's respect and praise. Mr. T's classroom difficulty was solved, and he had more to celebrate and reflect as a result. Alane tried the first idea, and Nick responded by sharing, so even more positivity could be reflected on the whole team. Notice that Mr. T said nothing to Nick about a problem. He just kept right on creating and pursuing the positive, and kept all the responsibility—and all the glory—for problem-solving with the students. Problem becomes triumph!

Here are more examples of relentless positivity, where a potential negative is flipped into a positive:

- Kendra raised her hand. When Ms. G called on her, Kendra said, "I've been in time-out *way* more than a minute!" Ms. G apologized for missing Kendra's success at completing her time-out, but went even further: "You showed me how motivated and assertive you are by speaking up so that you could get back into participating in class. What an achiever!" Many teachers would thank Kendra for the reminder, but Ms. G flipped the complaint into an opportunity to enhance her student's inner wealth.

- Mr. Y came up with an ingenious way to present class rules. Before, he had simply read through the rules at the beginning of each class period. He began to present the rules as manifestations of awesome character qualities shown by students *as they followed those rules*. For example: "Ladies and gentlemen, it is your consideration and respect that make this class great and safe for everyone. Lania is showing her respect for others by wiggling her finger to get permission to leave her seat so that we don't have crowds and can move easily across the room." In other words: following the rules is part and parcel of your overall awesomeness, and the more rules you manifest and follow, the more awesome you must have been in the first place!

- Take the old problem of students talking to one another during work time, or even when they should be listening to the teacher. Some teachers want total silence; others allow a steady roar. Could there be a treasure buried in talking among students? Here's an example of flipping into the positive. Two students were hurriedly talking in low voices during a pause in Ms. H's discussion of steps needed to complete a project. She could hear that they were on-task with the topic and that their conversation was about clarifying some of the steps with one another. Ms. H said, "I love how you guys rely so much on one another rather than only relying on me and that you waited for me to stop for a second before talking between yourselves. Very respectful and thoughtful." Ms. H does many little reflections like this to encourage her students to rely on one another for help and guidance. In her classroom, talking between students usually happens because one student has the knowledge to help another one succeed. That's what Ms. H is after—not "control" of the room. Students running the class and teaching each other: the more of that she sees, the better!

## More Pointers and Examples to Help You Build Students' Inner Wealth

You aren't the only source of inner wealth in your classroom. Inner wealth can come from other students as well. An example: Mario's correct loud answer helps everyone ace a question. Mr. Y broadcasts, "Thank you, Mario, for answering that question correctly—and loud and clear. You can all thank Mario for his ability when you all ace this question on tomorrow's test."

Not only is inner wealth built up by recognizing what the student has within him, it is also built up by recognizing the student's positive impact on others.

A student in Mr. Y's class announced, "This is easy." Several other students agreed. Mr. Y said, "This is actually hard material. It's the many things you do as students that only make it seem easy." He then listed several skills and qualities students demonstrated.

Mrs. V, dealing with a disruption by Pete in the classroom: "You are all showing great respect for Pete by keeping your composure right now. Pete, you are someone other people respect." As she says this, she puts a consequence card on Pete's desk. Imagine—Pete is acting the fool, and he is labeled as respected by other students? Yes, because the other students are not feeding the fire and encouraging more antics from Pete. *It is indeed great respect when students do what they can to maximize success in others.* By labeling the lack of reaction by the class as respect, the teacher is helping Pete have a transformational experience. At the same time, the teacher is making it possible for the class to have a relationship with him based in respect and success. Good news for the class and for Pete.

Students need help recognizing and labeling positive relationship qualities as well as recognizing and displaying appropriate social interactions. By pointing out how Mario's loud answer helps everyone, and by describing the class as respectful of Pete, teachers can build powerful transformational connections for the entire class.

One of Tom Grove's favorite methods of building inner wealth came from the heart of Ms. S. She would often link students and their caretakers together in her praise, which she did purposefully because seven students in the class had a dad in prison and some other students were in foster homes. She would comment, "What you just did was very thoughtful and mannerly. That shows me someone has been raising you right and you respect them. I am going to call them and thank them and tell them how much I like having you in my class. Who should I call?"

Not only do we honor ourselves with superlative behavior, we honor others as well. Ms. S brought this out in many ways:

"Marsha, your braids are beautiful. You must have sat very patiently, and someone must have really wanted to do a very good job for you."

"Verlon, you always seem to know a lot about current events. It seems to me someone at your home must discuss what's going on in the world with you. They are helping you to be wise so you'll have a great future."

Ms. S helped students see how valuable they were just by highlighting ordinary events and the connections that compose them. The students would beam from deep within. Such is inner wealth. It is a treasure deep within us that everyone can see.

## Further Enhancing Inner Wealth: Credit Systems and Other Techniques

While the unwavering focus on building inner wealth and the complete forgiveness of problems are powerful intrinsic rewards for students, the approach can be enhanced using more tangible techniques. Adding some incentives may be very motivating to students who are really struggling with inner wealth or have very little of their own.

The classic celebration of inner wealth is the credit system described in Howie Glasser's first book, *Transforming the Difficult Child*. You will find a full description of it here in Chapter Seven.

At Tolson Elementary, the teachers give students recognitions through Tolson Tributes. Other schools use "Virtue Vouchers" or "Thank You" or "Caught Being Good" paper notes. Some variations of these notes have both a carbon copy that goes into a weekly school-wide or classroom drawing for prizes and a top copy that the student can take home to show off. Many teachers tell the students to write on the note the character trait for which they are being recognized or may even ask the students to identify and add a positive trait to their notes themselves.

At First Flight Elementary in Kill Devil Hills, North Carolina, the school counselor collaborated with a local radio station so that students themselves actually broadcast stories of other students' efforts to "use their power in positive ways."

One of the most powerful celebration methods Tom Grove has seen is phone calls to the parents—*during class!* The teacher has all his students' parents on speed dial in his cell phone. When something great happens, he calls the parent right then and there! After-school calls are still great, but the "in-room" benefit is hard to match.

One of our favorite examples of a classroom privilege technique is the teacher who created an official-looking "Junior Peacefinder" badge. Kids could use credits they earned for positive behaviors to purchase 15 minutes of wearing the badge, which entitled the student to go around the classroom giving other students compliments. Even though the privilege was costly, it was often sold out days in advance. It clearly made kids feel happy and powerful to give others recognition. Another win-win.

Relaying stories of inner wealth to other teachers, students and the administration also provides rich reward and celebration. These stories can be written up and published in school newspapers. In one very public display of celebration, a teacher had the student sit in the cafeteria while the teacher stood in line and got lunch for the student. Some students feel incredibly rewarded when invited to eat lunch in the teacher's room.

Showing so much self-control that you get to help the teacher is really special. Showing justice or fairness to others such that your teacher carries your book bag to the bus for you is extra-special. Taking an actual Polaroid snapshot of a special moment for the student to take home is spectacular. The old stand-by rewards and celebrations—like choosing from the toy chest, getting a snack, or earning stickers—can also be effective if you keep in mind that it is always more effective to have rewards and celebrations *based in rich relationship*.

Here are some ideas for rewards and celebrations that can be used at the whole-class level. Some are more appropriate for younger children while others might work for older students. Use this list as a launching pad to guide your own imaginings of wonderful ways to celebrate student success:

| | |
|---|---|
| Tiptoe tag time | Quiet art time |
| Paper airplane time | Free time |
| Pencil tapping time | Headphone time |
| Face making time | Extra game time |
| Penny flipping contest | Extra library time |
| Group story time | Extra recess time |
| Group appreciation fest | Playground time for the class |
| Free time | Making a puppet or a project |
| Group reading time | Work with clay |
| Note passing contest | Grumble and growl time |
| Sing-along contest | Chalkboard doodle time |
| Giggle fest | Game time |
| Chair switching time | |

## "Good Job"

The object is to create an entirely different, higher-order trajectory in the nature of the positive statements we make to children. It is so easy to come up with all manner of language when we describe problems. In comparison, when it comes to successes, our language is typically so skimpy. We tend to make vague statements like "thank you" and "good job" that leave children wondering what exactly they have been appreciated for.

Think of this section as a huge grocery store full of healthy, delicious alternatives to "thank you" and "good job" that you can use to recognize and praise your students' efforts, behaviors, and achievements. As you build this vocabulary of praise, you will become more and more skilled at building your students' inner wealth.

Taking language to the next level propels the child's growing sense of self. It gives the child much more information and vital proof that she has indeed been seen and valued, which leads to the knowledge that she can value herself. The "explained" compliment gives the child a clear and incontrovertible sense of "I can" and "I am capable."

## *Instead of "good job" or "thank you," try:*

- I love the way you are choosing to be cooperative.
- You are showing you have great ears; you are listening very well.
- I see the way you are paying attention to detail and I appreciate that skill.

- I like the way you are having consideration for others.
- You are using a low-level voice in the classroom and that is a helpful choice.
- I really appreciate how you are planning well...you are being very organized.
- I notice that you are using your time well and accomplishing a lot.
- You are showing real talent for this assignment in the way you are putting all these pieces of information together.
- You are acting creatively in a way that is giving your project flair.
- I really like how you are working to master this information.
- You are being very successful by using good teamwork.
- I like how you are looking out for others. That's a nice quality.
- I want to appreciate your talent for having unique ideas.
- You are being surprising in the kinds of wonderful ideas you are coming up with.
- I like the creativity you are using. You are being dazzling.
- Thank you for contributing to the happy mood in the classroom right now.
- It really looks like you are feeling the joy of discovery...congratulations!
- You are showing amazing forethought. I like how you trusted your inner knowledge that things would work out.
- You are being marvelous in how you are showing perseverance.
- I want to acknowledge how you are being dedicated to success.
- You have taken this project beyond my imaginings, and I am very impressed.
- You are being powerful in the way you are managing your emotions.
- You are bringing out the best in others.
- I like how you are making a hard task look easy.
- I appreciate how you are handling your strong feelings very well.
- I see that you are making great choices to get along nicely with your classmates.
- I like how you are choosing what's important. That shows excellent judgment.
- You are demonstrating magnificent thinking.
- That is a brilliant thought you are expressing!
- You are being eye-popping awesome right now by choosing to follow the rules.
- I like how you are showing zest by doing your best on this assignment.
- I like how you are acting in a spirited manner. You are inspiring others.
- I really like how you are going above and beyond expectations.

- You are exceeding expectations with a great attitude to boot.
- You are being inspiring in the way you are conducting yourself.
- You are being courageous to break away from the pack and do the work in a way that's true to yourself.
- You are being like sunshine to others.
- Your writing has made others feel good.
- You are being wise. That is a great quality that is coming across in your diplomacy.
- You are showing great curiosity, which is a great way to learn.
- I really like how you are respecting yourself and others.
- You are using your great mind to figure out how to be successful. Congratulations.
- You are showing an open mind to new ideas. I like that a lot.
- You seem to be seeing the big picture.
- That was a very insightful inference you just shared.
- That was a delightful deduction you just made to figure out the answer. Well done.
- That was a solid educated guess and it is correct. That is a very important skill.
- You are being diligent in monitoring your progress accurately.
- You are showing a quick mind for picking up this new and difficult material.
- I notice how you are finding new possibilities in the ordinary.
- I want to acknowledge the inner wisdom that is shining through in your class participation.
- I see your determination and the effort you have made.
- I really like the sense of inner beauty that comes through in this artwork.
- Excellent use of logic.
- I am enjoying the clarity of the words you use to express yourself.
- I like how you are channeling your excitement.
- I am admiring your contribution to the discussion.
- I appreciate the collaboration and helpfulness you are contributing to your group.
- Thank you for handling that situation in a gracious way.
- You are a real independent worker!
- I appreciate the kindness you are showing our new student.
- Thanks for showing your generosity.
- Thanks for using integrity. You made a great decision to help even though you did not have to.
- You have shown a wonderful sense of awareness in sensing the needs

of others.

- I want to acknowledge you for using your inner wisdom in making that good choice just now.
- The way you put those two ideas together shows how you are using great analytic skills in your problem solving.
- I appreciate the intelligence in your answer to the question.
- Thanks for showing good responsibility.
- Thanks for being so courteous.
- I like the passion in your artwork. It shows a lot of life force and beauty.

## More substitutes for "thank you" and "good job"

| | |
|---|---|
| Cooperative | Handling strong emotions |
| Great ears | Making great choices |
| Attentive to detail | Choosing what's important |
| Considerate | Magnificent thinking |
| Using a low-level voice | Brilliant thoughts |
| Planning well together | Being eye-popping awesome |
| Focused | Showing zest |
| Managing his/her time well | Acting spirited |
| Self controlled | Going above and beyond |
| Accomplishing a lot | Exceeding expectations |
| Showing real talent | Being inspiring |
| Acting creatively | Courageous |
| Good teamwork | Sunshine to others |
| Looking out for others | Being wise |
| Pulling together | Having great curiosity |
| Having unique ideas | Respecting yourself |
| Being surprising | Using your great mind |
| Being dazzling | Having an open mind |
| Making a happy mood | Seeing the big picture |
| Feeling the joy of discovery | Making an insightful inference |
| Showing amazing forethought | Making delightful deductions |
| Showing perseverance | Making a solid educated guess |
| Dedicated to success | Diligent |
| Showing imagination | Showing a quick mind |
| Being powerful | Knowing when to reflect |
| Bringing out the best in others | Finding new in the ordinary |
| Making a hard task look easy | A good friend |

## More substitutes for "thank you" and "good job"
*continued*

Trustworthy

A joy

Brave

Honorable

Attentive

Easy to like

Compassionate

Reasonable

Patient

Empathetic

Respectful

Inspiring

Admirable

Generous

Thankful

Forgiving

Inquisitive

A great example

Flashing a contagious smile

Appreciative

A helper

A scientist

A hard worker

Understanding

In possession of innate ability

Showing s/he has been raised right

Faithful

A source of strength

A leader

A shining light

An advocate

Gracious

Visionary

Just or fair

Hopeful

Positive

Tactful

Steadfast

Peaceable

Strong on the inside

Constructive

Productive

Genuine

Good hearted

Demonstrating integrity

Loving

A lighthouse

Clear-minded

Showing balanced thinking

Vibrant

Beaming

Discerning

Direct

Powerfully spirited

Committed

Deeply understanding

Dignified

## What Students Experience as You Build Their Inner Wealth

This process of building inner wealth creates rich relationships between teacher and students. Imagine this from the students' point of view. They experience an adult who is attentive and thrilled with them—who surprises them over and over with undeniable evidence that they are wonderful in many ways. This adult is just and plays by the rules; accepts that everyone has problems; and does not cast blame or shame or resentment.

When a teacher applies this approach, she is seen by students as rarely able to be manipulated, but also as forgiving, restoring, and faithful. She comes across as devoted to student success, no matter what. She demonstrates that she values students over the lesson by spending her time and energy offering positive recognitions to them.

The respect of students quickly builds for a teacher who is not upset, defeated, or deregulated by student problems. The students have the experience of being given limitless opportunities to succeed and getting all the glory when they do. They experience even the smallest success as worthy of celebrating. In turn, the child inevitably comes to value small successes internally—he learns to celebrate the *process* and not just the end result. What a gift: to be able to feel pleased with their efforts and to value the efforts of others.

When held in such esteem, students don't mind being held to high standards—particularly when the teacher benevolently treats them as fully capable of attaining those standards. A teacher who sees things this way is bound to be joyful. How could you not be when you look beyond behavior into heart, spirit, and character and continually use reflections of those aspects to enhance students' inner wealth?

The Nurtured Heart Approach is designed to support every child. It is particularly useful, however, with the most challenging or "hard to reach" children in your classroom. They are the ones who often are most lacking in inner wealth and who most need it to realize that they are a welcome and wonderful part of the world.

## Targeting: For the Child Who Has Been Deeply Hurt

Some students are very difficult to reach, having been severely affected by unfortunate past relationships. Their trust in others and in themselves has been shaken or maybe even destroyed. They may be especially hopeless, angry, withdrawn, dissociated, disenfranchised, or irritable, or they may have taken the position of class clown to a new extreme to deflect their pain. Some such students may just seem flat-out disinterested in others. For these students, a deep spiritual focus is very useful.

Students burned by relationships have been treated either as if they don't matter or as if they don't even exist. Others have been treated in severely conditional ways—they have had to behave in such a way or do certain acts just to stay alive or be spared intense verbal or physical degradation. These children have only been deemed "good" if they behave and perform in ways that violate their spirit and basic nature. For others, there has just been chaos. Students like these need to be restored and guided back to where they can attach to their spirits, so they can trust and love themselves again (or maybe for the very first time).

Children who have been damaged like this need to know and feel what many of us take for granted because it is so deeply embedded in us. We are referring to three main elements of being human:

1) You belong.

2) You are competent.

3) You are valuable.

Sometimes, you can look at these students and see one, two, or maybe all three elements missing in action. They spiritually *hurt*. Some have numbed themselves to nearly everyone and everything. By targeting these three critical aspects of what makes us enfranchised human beings, you can reach these students in a deep way—which you may need to do because "ordinary" reflections of inner wealth may bounce off them.

**You belong** involves sending lots of messages that say, in essence, "You belong here, with us, in this school, regardless of what you bring to the situation in the way of your past or your problems. You are part of the picture and meant to be part of it. There is nothing you can do to be cast out or turned away permanently. You are given grace. If you mess up or go away, you will be welcomed back. There is a tie of acceptance you cannot sever."

**You are competent** involves many factors: "You have what it takes to learn, to make friends, and make sense of things. You have accurate radar, intuition, and awareness. You are enjoyable and capable of entering into safe relationships with others. You can grasp the significance of events, make use of subtle cues, see viable possibilities, and protect your spirit. You can control yourself and create positive outcomes with others." In its simplest form, *you are competent* means "You are good and wonderful as you are. You were made good, made to be happy, and to share happiness with others."

**You are valuable** means saying to the child that "your opinions, feelings, and intentions matter to me and to others. Your actions matter and have value to you and to all others. You, just by virtue of being alive, deserve all honor, respect, and consideration. You are worthy of influence, kindness, time, and energy and need not try to earn these things. They are already yours. Your life has meaning."

To deliver these messages and promote restoration, we still use the three legs of the table as the main process. Strictness is most reassuring to such students, as it is so dependable and easily understood. Not leaking negative energy is restorative to them—it might be the first time they have been able to have problems without the problems being a relationship issue or what draws them into closeness and connection. Relentless pursuit of the positive builds hope minute by minute. All three, together, create a trustworthy environment of spiritual safety.

To convey that the student belongs, you can introduce him to everyone, put something of his up in the room, smile at him first thing, involve him in no-fail discussions, and trust him with something of yours once in a while. Never leave him behind or start without him. Make plenty of opportunity for him to be helpful to the class, but do not make a big deal of it. As for verbal messages, you can remark how you like him being present, how another teacher made a positive remark to you about him, or how another teacher appreciates his presence in her class. Do "drive by" observations ("nice handwriting"), or talk to him about something he did a few days ago so that he experiences a sense of belonging in the thoughts of others in positive ways.

At first, remember that you do *not* want to act overly thrilled and excited about him. He'll think you are crazy (because he is really worthless in his opinion), or that you are after him in a bad, exploitative way (since the mean people in his past were way too interested in every little thing he did and gave it way too much importance/energy).

Here are some guidelines for appropriately conveying the sense of competence to these students. Be patient. Firmly convey that you expect him to be capable. Hold him to the same rules as everyone else and don't let him slide when others aren't either. Never leak negativity. Ask him to assist others. In other words, treat him as no less and no better than anyone else. *If you treat him as damaged, he will be damaged further.*

Reflect to students like this that they are correct in their intuition and able to see between the lines, take a hint, plan ahead, be aware of implications, deduce, use inductive reasoning, and problem-solve. Let them try out solutions to their problems as hypotheses to be learned from. Reflect how they possess qualities that would make them a good friend and the skills to make friends. Be especially aware of their intentions and reflect how positive those intentions are. Assume good intentions. Assume they make sense even when acting odd. Assume they can control it.

"You are valuable" gets conveyed by being in the moment with the student, taking time for him, reflecting how his actions affect others in positive ways, enjoying him as he is, and making him useful. Tell him he is a need-to-know person, influential just by the way he listens ("Your thoughtful expression encouraged Bill to keep pursuing his line of thinking on this matter"), and has ideas worth hearing and deserving of attention. Find ways to honor him (note his birthday, recognize how his answering may help someone else think in a new way about the issue, pause just to consider what he is saying, and so on).

This is not Pollyanna stuff, or making things up about a troubled student just to make him feel better. Every interaction with the student must be based on absolute truth. It's as if we are taking a photograph of a child that has captured a moment, and then it is up to us to put that photo under the microscope and describe exactly what we see. And what we see we convey as neither half full, nor half empty, but totally full—the toll taker in action. The descriptions above are incisive ways of telling the exact truth of the moment.

There are many other ways to send these spiritual messages out and reconnect students to their own sense of wonderfulness. Another targeting technique is to *re-frame or re-label the problem into a useful skill*. For example: a student who fights can be given reflections of how she is strong on the inside, or strong in her will, or powerful in her beliefs. A student who insults others can be told that he is a keen observer and can really see into the inner workings of others. A student who is off-task a lot may be noticed as a keen observer of details and tiny changes in the room. The class clown might be reframed as one who can quickly see opportunity and the light-hearted side of things. Remember, however, that all three legs of the table must be maintained, so any student calling another a name or fighting will get a consequence. Just as Quin got both a detention and praise for accepting it honorably, you can praise and consequence simultaneously. Relentlessly pursue the positive.

Take these themes and repeatedly redirect the student into more positive uses of her talents. Remember, the more intense the student, the more intensity she has for positive endeavors. Remember as well that they are struggling to belong, to be competent at something, and to be valued. Like the pencil sharpener and the meat-loaf examples, break their actions down so you can find some useful skill or quality to redirect in a positive way. It will also help to separate their intentions from their methods. You can praise the intentions and consequence the methods at the same time.

## Redefining the Difficult Child: Enormous Potential for Inner Wealth

ADHD and other such diagnoses are at an incredible peak. In some schools, 10 percent of boys are on stimulant drugs for ADHD. That's an estimated 40-fold increase in the rate of stimulant medication use for this purpose since 1970.

A generation ago, a child who caused trouble, failed to get along with others, underachieved, and disrupted the classroom might have simply been regarded as a bad kid or might have been subjected to corporal punishment or shipped off to military school. Today, such a child is quickly diagnosed, categorized, and possibly medicated. A generation ago, the child who daydreamed, was shy, anxious, withdrawn, melancholy, had dramatic mood swings, or was extremely sensitive or needy was not generally seen as having a mental illness. More often, that child was seen as special, or shy, or creative, perhaps as having an artistic temperament, or at worst, odd or weird. Today, this child is likely to end up labeled as depressed, anxious, ADD, or bipolar—and drugged with medicines that have not been adequately tested for safety or effectiveness in children.

Preschoolers as young as two are being given dangerous antipsychotic medications for supposed bipolar disorder (how on *earth* can one diagnose a two-year-old with something so serious?), while children aged two to four are commonly prescribed stimulant medication for ADHD.

The use of meds has become a first response for many doctors and other adults. This impedes us from looking at the importance of relationship and spiritual factors in difficult students. When a spouse seeks help for depression because her partner is demeaning her, the obvious solution isn't to take antidepressants and ignore the marriage issues. Nor would any ethical or decent counselor tell that patient she ought to just seek a divorce. Counselors think of ways to help them develop a more fulfilling relationship; they try to create a workable balance that supports both partners. Similarly, if a child is having difficulty managing her intensity, we can think of *how to help her cultivate a more fulfilling relationship between herself and her intensity.*

The Nurtured Heart Approach creates a great marriage between children and their inner workings so that they can "save" themselves in the same way a couple might "save" their marriage. It all boils down to how well one can manage problems and create positive outcomes and whether the problems are within us or between us and another person.

Americans in general are increasingly besieged with messages to view any sort of emotional problem as mental illness and in need of a pill. At first blush, it seems easier to deal with the issues in this way. If a difficult child is "diagnosed" and treated with drugs, suddenly your classroom may seem like a more peaceful place. On the outside, the child might even seem more content. You have every reason to want this, and many educators have been drawn into this paradigm.

Some parents are more comfortable with this paradigm, too. In generations past, parents of troublesome children tended to be seen as bad parents who had done something wrong to make their child's behavior so impossible. Today's paradigm removes blame and pegs certain types of misbehavior as a brain disorder that isn't anyone's fault. But we believe that this paradigm is much more damaging than doctors or drug companies want you to know—and that at some point in the not-so-distant future, there will be a backlash.

Why? Although there is abundant evidence that stimulant drugs, antipsychotics, and antidepressants are much more harmful to children than most people know, that issue is beyond the scope of this book. What you need to know as a teacher is: *the diagnosis paradigm is harmful because it casts the child's intensity, high energy, and drive as a disease.*

We tell the child there is something wrong with her intensity, when the real truth is that it doesn't fit into the current system. There isn't a place for especially high levels of intensity, energy, and sensitivity in the average classroom. The child who doesn't toe the party line is seen as causing problems, not as manifesting a quality that may well be the fount of his greatness. When we squash it with drugs, or we label it as a pathology, we do that child and the world he lives in an enormous disservice.

Howie Glasser's book *101 Reasons to Avoid Ritalin Like the Plague* opens with a telling cartoon from Mike Peters' strip *Grimmy* (and reprinted with permission from King Features Syndicate): A mother in Elizabethan dress holds her similarly dressed toddler son on her lap. He's scribbling like mad with a quill pen on a piece of parchment, and the mother says, "I'm worried, doctor. All he does is write." The doctor replies "No problem, Mrs. Shakespeare, I'll just give him Ritalin and he'll be like every other normal average kid."

By medicating a child's intensity away, we demonstrate that we cannot handle his essential life force and that he can't be trusted to do so either. The child ends up caught between the feeling of being drugged (not to mention the side effects, which can include insomnia, symptoms of obsessive-compulsive disorder, tics or Tourette's syndrome, loss of appetite, and in the most serious cases with long-term use, possible brain atrophy and heart damage)[8]—and the instinctive desire to re-capture the gorgeous intensity that has always gotten him in so much trouble but has been a source of joy and aliveness for him.

Even if the child isn't medicated, the simple act of diagnosis can be disparaging. Being told that you have a mental illness that never goes away is probably going to feel less than inspiring. It can certainly become a liability, as in the sense that you feel "less-than" those who aren't "mentally ill." At other times, it could be seen as an advantage, such as when students use their ADHD or other diagnosis to get ex-tended time to take exams, do assignments, or to claim that they're being discrim-inated against for their "disease." This kind of advantage, however, is more about preserving one's limitations than about growing one's inner wealth.

Think back to the section "The 'Energy-Challenged' Child" in Chapter Two. Rather than thinking of intense or sensitive children as mentally ill, think of the in-credible, white-hot energy burning inside them. They have so much to offer, and they need to figure out how to manage their energy. The Nurtured Heart Approach is about teaching children to do this in a way that continuously accrues inner wealth. Building that inner account will give them the reserves to control and *be married to* their intensity, not divorce and divide themselves from it. It can be the difference between a great life and a marginal and depressed existence.

The Nurtured Heart Approach has systematically "cured" countless cases of ADHD. It has helped make impossible children into children who are a pleasure to have around. It is a viable non-drug alternative for childhood behavior issues that can make a classroom completely fall apart in the time it takes to open a lesson plan. There are plenty of testimonials in both of Howie Glasser's books that

---

8. If this sounds impossible to you—that such a widely used drug could actually be more dangerous than the public has been led to believe—we strongly recommend that you read *101 Reasons to Avoid Ritalin Like the Plague (Including One Great Reason Why it's Almost Always Unnecessary)*. It's available at the web site, www.difficultchild.com. You can also get great, current information on the dangers of psychiatric drugging of children at the web site of Peter Breggin, M.D., www.breggin.com.

show this to be true.

If we drop-kick the psychopharmaceutical approach, will we return to the old paradigm of blaming the parents or teachers when things go wrong with a child?

Not in this approach. There is no blame placed here. The culprits are not the parents, child or teacher. The culprits are the methods our society has had at its disposal. Normal methods fail with these children. And the harder you try to make conventional approaches work, the worse the situation will get. Guaranteed. Using the right tool makes all the difference. We believe that tool is the Nurtured Heart Approach.

## The Special Rewards of Building Inner Wealth in the Difficult Child

Difficult children immediately recognize that adults who are striving to build their inner wealth are offering a very different relationship than anyone else has. They have become superbly attuned to messages that they are no good and never will be. To them, adults are easily deregulated, defeated, or spitefully uncaring. Such children often end up filled with anger and hopelessness, feeling damned to a lifetime of failure.

They find that the easiest way to avoid those angry, hopeless feelings is to seek thrills and excitement, regardless of others' disapproval. If they can prove that no one else is any good either, and if they can figure out how to blame others for their own failures, they feel less worthless themselves. Thus, the failures are perpetuated and they are given more messages that they are worthless.

Often, when something isn't working for us, we keep trying the same thing, just with more energy. You know the saying from Alcoholics Anonymous: *The definition of insanity is doing the same thing over and over again and expecting the results to be different.* This is typical human behavior. We all do it. As the battery in the remote dies, we just keep pressing it harder and faster.

Difficult children are no exception, but their failure rate is so high that their soul is in a panic that nothing and no one will ever redeem them. If they are "good," people often treat that behavior like a fluke or else make some remark with the subtext, "Well, it's about time." The message is that they are STILL not good enough. Difficult children respond by trying to sell the idea that they're bad and don't care. Conventional methods sell that right back to them by continuing to confer relationship and energy for adversity. More hundred-dollar bills.

The Nurtured Heart Approach is a loud and consistent refusal to encourage "bad" children to keep on being bad. Even more, this approach tells them there is good about them; in fact, there is "greatness" about them! We can prove this to the child over and over. We break the old patterns and start them on their way to building inner wealth.

# Chapter Five

## *Fear and Consequences*

MR. Y WAS ONE OF MANY TEACHERS who had been completely discombobulated by the antics of Pete, a seventh-grader. Pete sang, yelled out, made faces, came to class late, did no work, and was a spectacularly funny class clown. Pete usually got a detention during every class period. He was often found wandering the halls, or at in-school suspension, or suspended from school. No one ever seemed sure whether he'd had his meds or not: the minute Pete walked into school, staff were assessing him and sharing their impressions of whether he might have taken his medications. Fear and dread spread like wildfire.

Mr. Y decided to create abundant opportunity for success and competence for Pete in class. Instead of avoiding this difficult student by just trying to make it through class with him, Mr. Y went right at him with total confidence in Pete's competence. If Pete did something goofy, Mr. Y asked him questions about the lesson. If Pete broke a major rule, he was treated like anyone else who had done the same (no greater consequences, no less). And any minor effort Pete made to do his class work brought a barrage of praise from Mr. Y. Pete was often asked to venture an answer—even if it was just a guess. Instead of expecting more of the same old behavior from Pete, Mr. Y began treating him like a fully competent student! He was fearlessly going to convey to Pete that Pete was valuable, enjoyable, and belonged in class.

Soon Pete was less bothersome to other students in class and generally less disruptive. He began to do class work. Later, he began raising his hand to answer questions. He ceased his clowning and stayed seated. Pete began to live up to Mr. Y's positive, unshakable expectations. Only by treating Pete as though he were fully competent was Mr. Y able to do what others surely thought to be impossible. Many others had fussed at Pete to be competent, but *no one* save Mr. Y gave the message to this student that he *was* competent. Mr. Y had set out to fearlessly, relentlessly validate this fact over and over.

It's such a confusing message when difficult children are treated like perpetual failures, but then told, "You COULD be good if you would only X...Y...Z..." How can they be good if they are accustomed to being treated and regarded as a perpetual failure, a fearsome threat, or someone that is simply put up with from day to day?

This is like setting a goal for Shamu to jump a rope held 25 feet above the water, on command, without any prior training. You could think, "Well, maybe a whale *can* do this." Or think as a pessimist might: "Whales won't do this on command," or "Whales will be whales—what the heck are we even doing here?" or "Shamu didn't take his meds today, so let's just hope we can do this tomorrow." The key to our approach is to find every avenue to make the worst student feel competent and valuable as a person. Success is the only option. This is a route worth taking.

*OK, OK, already*, you might be thinking, *I get it. Positive recognition. Expect competence. Put Shamu's rope on the bottom. Put rope everywhere. Learn to see competence and achievement in even the smallest movement toward good behavior and good learning skills. Teach inner wealth first, then move on to the lesson. Praise and praise some more. Praise with great detail and specificity.* If you are thinking like this, congratulations—you DO have it!

More precisely: you have one leg of the three-legged table going strong. You recognize the importance of positivity and how to create time-in for your students. However, to create a powerful time-in and transform your classroom, the other two legs have to be going strong as well.

We've focused heavily on that one leg of relentless positivity until now because it's often the most difficult concept for parents and teachers to grasp. It requires an enormous shift in perspective for most people—a transformation in how we see our students: who they are, what they can become. Although all three legs are crucial, that positivity leg is the one that sets the foundation for the other two. If you don't really GET that leg, your other two will never hold. Relentless positivity is the background upon which the picture of success can be painted in vivid color. By having the other two legs in place—strictness and un-energizing negative behavior—the picture of success is greatly intensified.

Efforts to set strict limits, which comprise the second leg, must be closely coordinated with inspired positivity and be of sufficient intensity. In this chapter, we address the pressing issue of how to set limits that are strict and clear, but not severe or punitive, without giving our relationship energy to problems—also known as leaking negativity (that's the third leg). We want methods of giving consequences that work to "reset" a child who is breaking rules without dimming the light of positivity in the process.

## Consequences: Right and Wrong Ways

We can't ignore problem behaviors. That would be a disaster, especially in a classroom setting. We need reliable and consistent consequences that the child comes to expect. We also need consequences that enable us to hang on to the positive mood and direction in the classroom.

That means clear consequences that require little of the teacher's energy. No warnings and no lectures, just brief, immediate consequences for breaking a rule—like a minor infraction in a sporting event, or the quick reset of a video game after the player has made a mistake playing the game. Remember that lecturing doesn't work. When we lecture, we're trying to instill values and respect for rules at the time the child's receptivity is at its lowest, and we're handing over those energetic hundred-dollar bills as payment for negative behavior.

For the difficult child, warnings, lectures, second chances, and even punishments function as rewards. For example, consider the child who is sent to the office, where she receives lots of words and relationship from adults who are trying to get her to straighten up and fly right. Paradoxically, the child feels rewarded here, even as she feels like a failure. In this upside-down, "Stop-doing-that-here's-a-hundred-bucks" world, even the kindest heart-to-heart—although cherished as desperately needed recognition—encodes as failure.

Most of you can probably name students who consider in-school suspension, being sent to the office, or even out-of-school suspension as more desirable than class. They get to see their friends, have special one-on-one conversations with the most powerful people in the school, and might possibly pick up some office gossip while they wait to be chastised. They end up with a great tale to spin. Yet, for all their excitement and attention, these so-called consequences ultimately add up to failure.

Children learn early on that most adults (parents and teachers) always seem to have time for problems. A child who needs your time and energy will continue being drawn to problems as long as you pour your energy in that direction. This is where the importance of being very strict and not giving energy to problems becomes pivotal.

Drain as much energy, effort, emotion, relationship, and time as possible out of any response you give to a student's problem. Demonstrate that tantrums, fussing, pleading, arguing, or insults have no effect. Of course, there are some absolute rules and safety concerns that may have to be addressed, but even then, we want to give up as little energy, time and effort as possible. Think of a surgeon who has a patient with numerous serious injuries. The surgeon makes priorities and works his way to the best end possible. All the pleading, fussing, blaming, logic, admonitions, and reminding in the world will not patch the patient up. Surgery is just a time-out!

As soon as the time-out (consequence) ends, there is plenty of recognition and excitement for success—no grudges, no attitude that tells the student, "You're done screwing up for now, but I know it's just a matter of time before you screw up again." That attitude guarantees you more trouble and the student continued frustration and difficulty. It says, in the big picture, the student is not good.

For example, consider how common statements like the ones below actually serve as advertisements of our buttons that dare the student to push them. We are telling students how to have the most immediate and powerfully captivating relationship possible with us. We are leaking negative expectations and energy on problems that haven't even occurred yet. This is not what we mean by being strict.

"Don't you *dare*..."

"If I find out that you..."

"You better not..."

"Don't make me..."

"Are you crazy/stupid/trying to drive me insane?"

"Give me *one good reason* why you..."

We get just what we ask for when we inadvertently advertise to the child, "You are a failure, so here is exactly how you can fulfill my negative expectations of you." The child experiences that he is too much for adults to handle, which is a frightening realization. He begins to test adults to see if anyone *can* handle him. At some point, he falls into a panic, thinking that nothing can be done and that he might truly be no good and has no hope of turning things around.

Surely you've seen an expression of total relief wash over an out-of-control child's face when someone finally seems to figure out how to rein her in. Once that happens, the child can relax, knowing where the boundaries lie. As you apply this approach, be prepared to see that expression on the faces of your most difficult students.

Whatever your expectation, the child will comply. You'll see how true this is when you have the Nurtured Heart Approach up and running. When you expect the best, it's far more likely to shine forth from the child. However, it takes being strict, not leaking energy on problems, and pursuit of the positive to see these expectations materialize.

The right kinds of consequences play a big part in making the whole approach work. You use consequences to set limits and to show your students that they get far more of your energy and focus when they follow the rules, reflect appropriate values, and apply themselves to learning. Children figure out this new kind of consequence in no time and throw themselves into the game. By way of consequences, you demonstrate that the child now gets nothing from breaking a rule—aside from a result that is void of energy and relationship.

This having been said, it's also important to give students "permission" to break the rules. "What?" you might be thinking. "Permission to break rules? What on earth could those nurturing fellows be getting at now?"

We are so geared to see rule-breaking as a really terrible thing that should be avoided at all costs. Instead, we need to get out of the way and allow kids to experience what happens when they break a rule. If we constantly try to prevent rule-breaking, and if we continually focus our energy on persuading students to follow the rules, they will never have the chance to see that there is no longer any energy or relationship to be gained with negativity.

Besides, children do know the secret: that they can break rules any time they wish, even if they are on medications. We are fooling ourselves if we think we can stop them with admonishments and threats. These tactics put another log on the very fire we're trying to put out.

Adults have permission to break rules, too, don't we? What about rules that try to prevent us from swearing, from insulting others, from acts of aggression, from speeding or from violating any other of our society's conditions? The truth is that we have the freedom to break these any time we wish. We might get caught and have a consequence, but we also always have permission to see what really transpires when we cross the line.

**By realizing that it's a child's choice not to break a rule, we are in a far better position to appreciate the effort involved** and not just take it for granted. We are in a far better position to see the line being crossed and to respond by effortlessly issuing a consequence.

## The Time-Out, Nurtured Heart Approach-Style

Different schools of thought exist on what kind of consequences work best to stop negative behaviors while preserving the child's confidence and desire to do good. The ones commonly used in schools and at home are time-outs, natural/logical consequences (the child suffers the natural consequences of his own misbehavior), the removal of privileges (no recess, no computer time, no TV), or giving extra work (writing or other assignments).

All of these things are, in essence, typically used as some type of punishment to teach the child a lesson. Some children are able to benefit from any of these consequences; in other words, they learn to improve their behavior. However, when these methods do not work, adults may find themselves intensifying these consequences. If a little punishment didn't work, maybe a lot will. In the Nurtured Heart Approach, we are not after punishment so much as a quick "reset" that gets the student back into experiencing success again as quickly as possible. We call it a time-out, but it is truly a form of "reset" and we use these terms interchangeably along with other terms like "chill" or "pause."

In our parenting and teaching culture, the time-out has become the consequence of choice, so we'd like to offer a format of time-out that we believe works best. We do *not* recommend natural/logical consequences, removal of privileges, or extra work. Our proven method of choice is a short, simple, straightforward time-out, or "reset."

We create the result we need in the moment, which is to pause the child when he is breaking a rule, but we then can move the child quickly into more success. This is where the awakening happens; it does not happen during the punishment and won't sink in more with escalating consequences. The awakening happens during the time-ins that come right on the heels of the time-outs. Removing privileges encourages the distorted logic that if a small loss of privilege doesn't work, maybe a larger one or even the removal of a more valued privilege will...and you're in a downward spiral, leaking increasing amounts of energy into problems.

With very short "resets" that direct the child right back into success, you are handing out the least amount of energy along with maximum strictness. This way of giving a consequence puts the teacher in a more empowered position to move through the situation to a new space where things are going well.

Time-outs work because virtually any child wants, more than anything, to be in the game, to remain in the loop of human interaction. Even those who resist interaction mightily are, in reality, so hungry for it that they don't quite know how to handle it when it comes their way.

For teachers who have never used what we call the "clean" time-out, shifting to this mode of consequences can be a source of major anxiety. Usually, we ask teachers to just stop whatever they have been doing for consequences and begin using time-out. This scares the daylights out of some of them! "What if the students refuse?!? These are tough children...these are eighth graders, for goodness sake!" Truth be told, it's always a shock to the students, but *they do it*. This is another of those phenomena that Tom Grove saw clearly during many classroom applications of this approach—i.e, that *students are always compliant with expectations*. It's like swallowing a pill: if you think you'll choke, you do, but if you have your mind made up to swallow it, you do. Don't fear your fear; feel it, and *approach* what you fear.

On the other hand, numerous teachers just start doing clean time-outs with no hesitation. We were particularly impressed with the way one student teacher immediately introduced time-outs and applied them. The teacher explained that he was going to start giving "resets" to students for breaking a rule and went on to list several ways that the students would benefit from resets, as opposed to the usual detentions or trips to the office. He explained that they would still be able to hear the lesson and stay smart; their parents would not have to be notified about the infraction; and they would be allowed to take care of the problem on their own. They would be able to get right back into opportunities to hear more positives about themselves. Only one student had a comment of any kind, which the teacher handled by recounting positives for the student. This introduction to the reset method was done with only four weeks of school left, and the class changed for the better that very day.

Bottom line: there is no special moment or timing for introducing clean time-outs. Whenever you begin, the benefits become immediately reinforcing to the students. They welcome it.

Time-out can be done in many ways. Some teachers have students put their heads on their desks. (This helps the teacher remember that the student is in time-out.) Others have students scoot their chairs back, and others simply have students sit where they are in the moment and be quiet and still. While a student is in time-out, no work counts, no questions are answered, and no one is to talk to the student. For very young students in preschools and kindergarten, a reset can be a simple pause.

As we've said, the Nurtured Heart Approach uses a "clean" version of time-out when a child breaks the rules. What is a "clean" time-out? Well, it's quite different from the version that is tried and discarded by most parents of difficult children. Typically, a time-out is given along with a hefty helping of lecture and reprimand. A lot of energy and relationship are delivered along with the time-out—another example of telling the child he's being bad, then energetically slipping him a hundred bucks.

The clean time-out may last two seconds, but no more than a minute. Yes...you read that right—two seconds to a minute is plenty of time as long as a lavishly positive time-in is waiting on the other side.

***Time-out is not a punishment!*** It's a silent "oops, check yourself!" message...without the discussion. It's a reset. It's a meta-message to the student that he has an opportunity to control his impulses without us stating or demanding that directly. Don't discuss the problem; don't take away prior credit; don't get into any discussion about whether a rule was actually broken. It's over. Back in the game! Start recognizing student success.

If the problem happens again, then yet again it's a time-out and another opportunity to get in control. And if the problem doesn't recur, then it's our opportunity to celebrate that as a success with the student. The door is then wide open to make a big deal over the positive side of the coin. This is all three legs working in concert.

One mother commented that her son's teacher did not want to use time-out because it might be "humiliating" for the student to be "singled out" from everyone else. Remember that in this approach, mistakes are no big deal; you don't leak energy on the time-out, and this consequence is quickly followed by what is hopefully a hugely rich time-in—the presence and confirmation of inner wealth. Every student has to follow the same rules, and everyone gets a time-out if one is broken; it simply serves as a kind reminder of the rules. There's no humiliation when everyone is accorded the same treatment. Every sport has a referee who singles out and consequences players when rules are broken, and players don't act humiliated by this; they expect it, if not welcome it. The tighter the game is called, the more intense it is, and the more exciting it is for the fans and the players. Children know when a rule is broken and expect a result.

One beauty of this approach is its emphasis on providing "warnings" by appreciating the success of the child when rules **aren't** being broken. These appreciative comments serve to let the child know with certainty that the rules are still the rules. The teacher knows that the students know, and students know that the teacher knows. **The rules, in essence, are removed from the relationship between you and students; the rules are just the way it is and not a topic for negotiation or debate.**

Thus, the *enforcement* of the rules does not become part of your relationship, either. The strict enforcement of rules becomes expected...and this, believe it or not, will be a great relief for students who are frustrated by inconsistent consequences or lack of consequences altogether!

A student may need several time-outs in one class period. A student can get many per class period and all is well as long as he does them. Refusal to do a time-out calls for further action, however. Some teachers give a detention and others call the home. In a severe case of disruption and refusal, the student may be sent to the office.

Some students want to test the teacher in any way possible to see if the teacher will blow up or break down. If you keep all three legs strong in the process, you are succeeding fabulously. If the student tests you this way, you know he is feeling the challenge to shift his internal belief from "no good" to something far more positive. He is trying to drive you to spew negativity to reconfirm that he is no good in order to remain in his previous comfort zone. One way he can do this is to violate major, district-wide rules of conduct. The student may think, "Oh sure, you can keep your cool and be positive when I have minor problems, but I bet you're just faking that you think I'm good. Here, I'll prove it by doing some serious, major rule-breaking."

If you remain true and solid with all three legs, you will have to abide by those rules of school policy, which may demand that you send the student out. However, you have shown the student that he cannot violate the relationship! By maintaining the relationship qualities, you have succeeded tremendously at giving him even more of a challenge to his inner belief. These steps are usually unnecessary if the teacher is patient, firm, and not leaking negative energy. More importantly, they are unnecessary when the teacher continues to convey that she sees positives in what the student is doing right in that very moment and that she still sincerely wants the child in the classroom.

In the big picture, it is highly desirable for students to test this new approach. They develop a firm, experience-based understanding that there's no longer anything to be gained through negativity. That's where the transformation takes place and that's when the student's investment of his intensity into success gets greater.

Time-outs should always occur in the classroom and not elsewhere, except when school policy dictates differently. Schools that fully adopt this approach make a policy that consequences can be administered in the classroom. This allows the teacher to reset the child to success, which is the real agenda, and avoid the major problem of sending the child out of the room. When a child perceives herself as "exiled," along with it comes the impression that the teacher cannot handle her. When the child comes back to the room, she is likely to test—usually in stronger ways—to assess whether the teacher is better able to handle her now.

Another common mistake made with the typical time-out happens when we haven't sufficiently set up the time-in. Remember that time-in is where we create the child's perception of the flow of energy and relationship when things are going right. Time-in offers emotional and psychological nutrition—an essential counterpoint to the time-out. The time-in is a flood of positivity and energy that is restored right on the tail of the time-out—and, of course, before rules are even broken at all. Essentially, the time-in is anytime the child is not in time-out, when you are recognizing positives and building inner wealth. A time-out cannot be clean or meaningful under this approach unless you are enveloping the child in time-ins.

Some time-outs are imposed without a word. A gesture can be given to signal the issuance of a time-out. Most often, all that students are told is "[their name], reset or time-out." When several students are breaking a rule at once, you can try this: "Everyone talking right now needs to show me your honesty and put yourself in time-out." Both authors have seen this work a hundred times, and it also presents a bonus opportunity for you to praise honesty! (Only do this if you know which students are involved; a guess may prove wrong and result in an erroneous consequence.)

Here are a few pointers for giving effective time-outs:

- Be strict but not stern. Remember, students' poor behavior doesn't throw you. The rules are the rules; that's just the way it is. You certainly desire for your students to follow the rules but you are not offended when a rule is broken. The child perceives you as not being attached to the problem. Imagine a state trooper stopping you for speeding, yelling at you about it, and then sending you to his command post to be yelled at some more by his supervisor. We'd think the trooper and his supervisor have lost their marbles and gone way beyond their job of issuing us a ticket. Why should we treat rule-breaking by children any differently than we would expect to be treated in a similar situation? Or imagine a referee in a basketball game fussing, frowning, and shaking his finger at a player. What he's supposed to do is blow the whistle for every infraction on a consistent basis; give out the consequence; and then everyone's back in the game.

- Don't lecture the child or give her any other energy on the way to or while she is in time-out. Even two seconds can be enough time. If you are energizing success, she'll quickly see that success is far more interesting than a boring time-out.

- Use a calm, normal tone of voice and give the time-out as unceremoniously as possible. Give the student a little bit of time to accept the time-out; don't nag or pressure—that's handing out more hundred-dollar bills. No need even to say what the broken rule was—the child knows! If she isn't sure, she has the option of breaking the rule again in the future as a way of being certain. The teacher need say nothing more than "time-out" (and the child's name, if necessary).

- Don't let the child rope you into a battle over the time-out. Ignore any display of bad attitude the child exhibits in response to a time-out, and definitely don't add time to the time-out as a consequence for those kinds of displays. Just enforce the one original time-out. If the child escalates, simply come back when even a moment of calm ensues and confront the child with the truth of that new moment. "Hal, I see you are trying to get back into control despite being upset. That shows excellent judgment." Celebrate the victory because the battle could have continued and it was really the child's choice to bring the battle to a close. If the child acts out again, stay with the truth of this next moment by giving another time-out. Our power comes from a willingness to be in the truth of the current moment.

- We do not recommend designating a special place or area for time-outs. Doing so merely presents the possibility that the student refuses to go to that place, exacerbating the situation. It also can cause disruption for the class while the student puts on quite a show on his way to time-out. Remember that your goal is to have as little fuss and time spent on the problem as possible.

- When the student completes time-out, take the opportunity to point out another success. "Wow, Tyler, you sat so well through that time-out. I appreciate that you were able to accept the consequences of breaking a rule, even though you were angry. Terrific inner power!" Do this even if you had to struggle to get him there.

- DANGER! Be sure you are giving way more recognition to this student for his successes at other times or he will want to get time-outs just to get praised.

- If you want to turn the time-in (following the time-out) into a teachable moment, or if you are just itching to give a lecture about why the child got the consequence, wait a moment after the child is back in the game, then comment: "Tricia, I love that you are choosing to work quietly now. You are showing self-control even though you are still angry about the time-out." This way, you are re-establishing the time-in and getting back to pursuit of the positive while also stating your point. Give the "lecture" of celebration, make a "fuss" of positivity, but do it when things start going right and you will best make the points you wish to make and be influential in a positive way.

- KEEP TIME-OUTS SHORT! We cannot emphasize this enough. The time-out essentially is an interruption of the problem—a diversion—more than it is what society would have us view as a punitive consequence. Keep reminding yourself that the clean time-out does not depend upon the level of severity to have its impact. A longer time-out is not going to wield more impact than a short one. The goal is always to divert the situation directly into the next series of successful moments.

## Common Pitfalls to Avoid When Giving Time-Outs

1 Giving a time-out but not finishing it. In other words, forgetting to gain closure by notifying a child that the consequence has been successfully completed.

2. Giving the student control over ending the time-out.

3. Allowing a student to make contributions to the lesson while breaking a rule or in time-out (a very common stumbling block for teachers who are pushing the academic curriculum over the social curriculum).

4. Explaining to the child or to the class what the infraction was or any other way of inadvertently giving energy and relationship to the problem.

5. Being offended by the rule that was broken or in any other manner demonstrating that it was taken personally.

6. Doing things that contribute to the child's old portfolio of feeling most celebrated for his problems. This can inadvertently happen by seeking apologies or promises to never break the rule again or by trying to mediate the problem with others.

7. Giving the consequence in a way that is shaming or humiliating.

8. Forgetting to take the child right back into time-in by celebrating the child's successful completion of the time-out or any other behavior that can be praised.

9. Giving a time-out when a rule looks like it will be broken but hasn't actually been broken.

10. Looking the other way and choosing to avoid giving a time-out when a line has been crossed.

11. Giving warnings or re-direction, which are really more evidence of energy and relationship in the context of negativity.

12. Recognizing a student for every infraction without offering that student even greater recognition of successes.

Applying the concepts that support the three-legged table enables us to re-direct children's intensity rather than divorcing them from it. We are not communicating that they should "stop the bad stuff." Instead, we are boldly highlighting how often they are successfully managing their intensity in wonderful ways. You can have a wonderfully joyous, positive relationship and be gainfully influential with students even on days when rules are being broken!

As some students have told Ms. N, you can be "the nicest mean teacher" anyone ever had. Again, this comes from the powerful combination of all three legs. When the rules are the rules, and not part of the relationship, you can re-direct a student's intensity via numerous brief time-outs while super-soaking him in positives for his successes, however brief those successes might be.

On one hand, you are relentlessly enforcing rules; on the other, relentlessly reflecting many outstanding qualities the student is evidencing at that very moment. You are not really mean at all—just strict and matter-of-fact about the rules. You are not telling the student overtly or covertly that he is too intense and needs to suppress his intensity; you are teaching him to reset himself for moments where he is successfully channeling that intensity.

Similarly, you are not really being "nice" either—at least in a conventional way. You are reflecting evidence of wonderfulness, like a scientist observing and reflecting on the human spirit—simply abiding by the truth of each next moment as it unfolds.

For example: Mr. Y gave Joe numerous time-outs, yet he always thoroughly enjoyed the times when Joe was acting like a great student and citizen. Mr. Y was clearly showing Joe that he belonged—that he was valuable, enjoyable, and ultimately competent.

Some students may find character praise to be too overwhelming at the outset. Some may love the praise, but get too excited by it and wind up breaking a rule. Others have been exploited and do not trust attention from adults so they look at it as a setup. Begin with these students by praising at the "good job" level and gradually move into transforming levels of appreciation, recognition, and acknowledgment. The way through the trust and testing issues is *more* positives, not less.

## Don't Say "Thanks" When Time-Out Ends

Thanking a student for completing a time-out implies that the student has done something that makes you happy or pleases you in some way. This is not actually rule enforcement. When students are given a time-out, it is a consequence they need to serve, not a favor they are doing for you. Saying "Thank you for doing your time-out" implies that they've done you a favor.

What you can do after time-out is over is reflect something about the student that she can be pleased with. You may wish to:

- acknowledge the student's self-control or her ability to redirect herself
- acknowledge her maturity in accepting the consequences of her actions
- acknowledge her for completing the consequence with a good attitude
- tell the student that she helps the entire class be successful by getting on task so fast
- tell the student that her quick acceptance of her time-out puts her back in a

position to make great contributions to the learning that is going on.

Just be sure to pour out recognitions at other times she is being successful, too, not just after breaking a rule. Otherwise, she will break rules to capture your positive energy.

## More Time-Out Tips

In some very difficult classrooms, we have seen teachers trying to establish the Nurtured Heart Approach with one small group of students at a time, using a low voice or speaking quietly to individual students. They were doing well at celebrating student success and enforcing the rules, but it was on too small a scale. It wasn't until these teachers got up front, started keeping their eyes on the whole class for the majority of the time, and included everyone as an unavoidable presence that the classes improved. The students realized that they no longer had to try to engage the teacher out of her small, traveling sphere of relationship with loud, disruptive behaviors. Their quiet success became sufficient to readily capture relationship with the teacher.

When you first begin using time-outs, they should be delivered at a voice level that everyone will notice. Not loud (in a "you're totally GETTING TO ME" way), but in a matter-of-fact way. Fearlessly enforce at a level at which every child in the room can be aware. Remember, the rules are meaningful to you but you do not take it personally when a rule is being broken. The rules are just the way it is. Another way of looking at this is to say that the teacher should let every student know that there is potential for instantaneous relationship with the teacher, no matter where they are in the room—not just in a four-foot circle around the teacher.

Give positive recognitions and praise at a voice level everyone will notice as well, but with more energy than you put into the time-outs. The more you are giving consequences, the higher your rate of positive relationship needs to be with the class in general. *Never surrender your emphasis on the success of those doing well.* During those difficult moments where the room is starting to dissolve, avoid running around the room putting out fires. Start firing positives out there as fast as you can.

When things are going well, *don't back off of the positives*. If you use positive recognition only to suppress bad behavior, you'll get more bad behavior, because students will see through the positives as just another tactic to get them to behave.

Sometimes we have observed other students in effect giving the equivalent of a time-out. For example, in a science class of 21 students, six did nothing productive for two days. They spent the class time chatting and disregarded everything else. On the third day, the teacher sent productive students to the computer lab one by one until only the six remained in the room. They chatted away for about 10 minutes (!) before one noticed how empty the room had become. "Hey!" she exclaimed. "Where did everybody go?" The teacher shrugged and asked, "Where could they be?" The students figured it out and all but one started working without a word from the teacher. The last student continued her refusal to do any work for the next five days of class. She would wander about, trying to engage whomever she could in conversation, to no avail. On the sixth day, she slammed her book open on the table as she sat down to read. She worked every day thereafter. She had been put in a very effective time-out by her peers! Her peers had been put in a very effective time-in by the teacher, and they chose that relationship over the one being offered by the girl who was not working. Of course, the teacher gave those students recognition for their diligence, focus, and wise choices.

Somehow, our culture has come to believe that a consequence has to be drastic in order to work. If it isn't punitive, if it doesn't hurt the child in some significant way, most of us believe that it just won't be effective in changing the child's ways. There is a certain logic to this, and adults can sometimes scare children into acting the way we want them to. But telling a child what NOT to do, what NOT to be, leaves him empty; ever-escalating consequences and threats of consequences leave him feeling angry and/or fearful, oppositional, or like a failure; and theoretical, abstract discussions of values he SHOULD reflect leave him confused.

We have found time and time again with this approach that real awakening happens through the avenue of success, not through punishment. A problem is not the big deal it is normally deemed to be because we know in advance we will move through that stage when the experience of success becomes the really big deal! That's where the child's awakening (or enlightenment) happens in the deepest, most joyous, most constructive way. When children come to like the feeling of success and the internal sense of strength and thriving that comes with it, they clearly reinvent themselves to live their lives in successful ways. That's inner wealth.

## About Warnings

Have you noticed how well intense children can play video games? All they want to do is go to the next level, striving tirelessly for mastery and accomplishment. These games give the child permission to break rules and give no warnings whatsoever; they just issue the consequence when a line is crossed even fractionally. Although the consequence may look drastic, who's back in the game in a second or two?

Some may argue in favor of warnings on the basis that some students seem incapable of remembering the rules or that they cannot be held responsible for their own behavior because they aren't able to control themselves. As soon as we make these arguments, our standards have fallen—and with them falls our opportunity to maximize inner wealth. If students can follow the rules and be timed-out without warning during a basketball game in Phys Ed, they can follow the same guidelines when sitting at a desk. Besides: Warnings are laden with energy and relationship and reward negativity. In addition, warnings may not be as compassionate as tradition would have us believe. If a teacher is having a good day, he may give more warnings before a consequence than he might if he were having a bad day. This is an example not of compassion but of confusion. With the Nurtured Heart Approach, we are aiming to replace confusion or mixed signals with consistency and fairness.

Mr. C asked Tom Grove for help because he faced a madhouse every day after lunch. His students were supposed to come in and do a "warm-up" to transition to a calmer place from the excited, intense relationships they have at lunch. But in reality, the children would run in and out of the room, yell, and sometimes punch or harass each other. Even with two aides, it was at least 15 minutes before any order appeared, and that order tended to be brief.

Mr. C began his process of recognizing positives and plugging leaks of negativity. The school policy dictated that students be given a warning before a consequence, so Mr. C implemented a creative "warning" procedure. The first warning took place at the beginning of the class period when Mr. C would point to a list of rules or ask students to name one rule. He would praise students for knowing and reciting a rule, then say, "OK, class, that's your first reminder." With this reminder (warning) out of the way right off the bat, he could give consequences immediately thereafter as needed. His room became much more orderly. This became Mr. C's favorite class. In fact, this was another group of students who one day realized what a great class they were and spontaneously applauded themselves.

## Strictness and High Expectations

For proper rule enforcement, you'll need to thoroughly grasp the meaning of the word "strict" to make this approach work as well as it can. Strictness is one of the legs of our three-legged table, so it is critical for supporting the table. In this context, it means that we *keep the standard of desired behavior very high,* and we never waver when it comes time to enforce a rule.

If you find yourself repeating a rule, it's time to start enforcing it. If you don't enforce it every time, it isn't a rule. If you find yourself thinking, "These kids have forgotten the rules," you probably need to be stricter in your enforcement of those rules, as well as amp up your celebration and recognition of rules *not* broken. Keep "nailing" students for even the smallest degrees of appropriate effort, attitude, and action.

As a teacher, think in terms of the absolute best that you want socially (not academically) from your students. Imagine the ideal classroom, the ideal student, the ideal mood of the room. Hold this as your specific goal. Then, hold everyone to this standard. In everything you do—giving recognition, enforcing rules, and teaching—this standard should be as obvious as the sun in July.

Approaching strictness in this way lets you forget about students' histories. Everyone is held up to the same standards, regardless of what has happened in their lives in the past.

Ms. H had a new student, Richard, who talked constantly and popped in and out of his chair. Richard was so hyper that even the other children would ask him to stop or tell him to shut up. "I can't help it," he told everyone. "I got ADHD and have to take Ritalin and Trazedon. I hate it!" Ms. H simply began to point out every time he was able to sit still. No conversation took place about his 'condition' or his past behavior. No excuses were made for him. Just two weeks later, Richard was "doing beautifully" in class. All of his self-loathing and anguish seemed gone, and he was sitting calmly at his desk.

Richard's expectations were changed by the teacher's expectations. High expectations are an embodiment of the relentless pursuit of positivity. Students recognize this right away—it stands out like a neon sign, particularly for children who are so used to being met with negative expectations from easily defeated, frustrated adults.

Make students as responsible as you can. Make them think as much as possible. Let them know you are counting on them to address and solve their own their problems—and then make sure they experience success when they do. Let them know they can figure things out, they are competent at navigating their life, and that you have respect for them. All very high expectations.

In Ms. P's classroom, at least four of her students forgot their books every day. She told other students to share their books, until one student piped up, "I'm not sharing my book with him! I remembered mine, and he can remember his, too!" Ms. P became upset with the student for being unwilling to share. Major negativity was being leaked in response to unwanted behavior. After observing this scenario, Tom Grove helped Ms. P set up the following rule: If you forget your book, you cannot share and you cannot use extra books (they were removed from the classroom). You could sit without a book and do the best you could, or you could go get your book from your locker in exchange for a tardy. Ms. P consistently enforced this rule, and within a week, everyone was bringing their books to class. Everyone who remembered their books got "Thank You" notes. Ms. P needed to make the students responsible for their books, then engage in rich, positive relationship with them when the books showed up in the classroom.

Notice that Ms. P did not have a talk with students about ways they could remember or remind themselves about their books. She simply set a very high expectation with a clear rule—in this case, a choice—but a rule nonetheless. Her students rose to the level of expectation.

We have seen many classrooms that have come a long way since the Nurtured Heart Approach was instituted. We have also seen some that still struggle. This can usually be attributed to one of the following:

1. *The teacher's rate of recognitions is too low.* When the rate of positive recognitions from the teacher falls too far below the student's rate of interaction, the

relationship is not potent enough to cause transformation.

2. *The teacher is not using powerful character recognitions.* Recognitions that convey a vague notion of "good job" pale in comparison to ones that convey to the child attainment in relation to respect, wisdom, being thoughtful and making good choices. Appreciations that are conveyed in the context of an "irrefutable" real life experience become even more convincing to the child. Another possibility is that the recognitions may be too group-oriented instead of student-specific.

3. *The teacher is leaking negativity.* If the teacher is being positive yet also periodically leaking out negative energy on problems, the students remain unsure where the most relationship energy is.

4. *The teacher is too vague about rule enforcement.* The rules aren't being clearly, consistently, or strictly enforced. Students then take the chance that there is more relationship to be had through difficulty and sometimes find it true.

## When to Give a Consequence, When to Ignore

Adults working to implement the Nurtured Heart Approach often become confused about when to give a consequence and when to simply ignore a behavior. In *Transforming the Difficult Child,* the concept of ignoring a negative behavior isn't even an option, but in a classroom setting with 20 or more kids, it can be an impossibility to consequence every broken rule. The same may be true for a parent who is interacting with one very challenging child or more than one child at a time. Is there some way of prioritizing which behaviors ought to be subject to consequences and which can be allowed to slip by?

Ideally, you should give a consequence for every broken rule if at all possible. In some very difficult classes just starting the approach, it is not uncommon for five to 10 students to be in time-out at the same time. Sometimes an entire room will be in time-out at once!

Does ignoring certain rule-breaking behaviors make the adult inconsistent? What will the other students think if the teacher lets one student slide on some behaviors? Does it undermine the leg of strictness in our oft-mentioned three-legged table to ignore some behavior? Some who are learning the approach remark that, if there's no pre-established rule against a behavior, they shouldn't deliver a consequence. They feel it is unfair to students to not let them know ahead of time what the rules are. Should they have a bunch of pre-set rules from the get-go, and refrain from administering a consequence for rule breaking until it has been added as an official rule?

Before we go down that slippery slope, we'd like to make clear that the answers to these questions can be found in the basic principles of the approach. As long as these basic principles are in place, many options are possible for your particular situation—like Mr. C's solution to warning students in advance per the school policy. As you read through the examples and discussions that follow, we believe you will see that you can still adhere to the principles of the Nurtured Heart Approach while making it work best in your classroom situation.

- Bill walked into class late, which was okay because he had a pass. However, he immediately got in front of Mr. S, halfway raised his hand, and uttered a few words. Mr. S ignored him and continued to focus on praising the rest of the class. Bill raised his hand higher and waved it around a bit, but was still ignored. He walked a little closer to his seat but knelt in another student's chair and waved his hand even higher. Still, nothing from the teacher. Next, he tried sitting fully in the other student's chair with his hand up. When that didn't work, he finally went to his own chair, sat down, and raised his hand. Bingo! Bill was called upon.

- Curtis was acting up and being disruptive. He was refusing time-out, talking loudly, and disrupting the whole class. Rapid positive reflections seemed only to provoke escalations of the negative behaviors, undoing the brief glimmers of positive behavior. Curtis was going to the mat in this match and trying with all his might to extract some negativity from Mrs. N. After about 20 minutes of this battle, Mrs. N calmly handed him a discipline referral, and he went into the hall to head to the office. A few minutes later, another teacher poked her head into the classroom to tell Mrs. N that Curtis was still in the hallway. When Mrs. N went out the door to send Curtis to the office, she noticed he was crying...and doing his class work! He wanted another chance, and the teacher agreed to give him that chance. He was praised for redirecting himself, being courageous enough to believe in himself, and making wise choices. There were no admonitions, lectures or warnings. He was successful for the remainder of the class.

**Relentless pursuit of the positive:** In these examples, the two students and teachers were—either from the beginning, or in the end—pursuing the positive. Bill was making some movement toward his seat and Curtis had fully redirected himself out in the hallway. As long as the student is not escalating, no rule is being violated in the present moment, and the student is making steps toward compliance, the best way to pursue the positive is to ignore the student until the desired outcome occurs. Bill got in his seat, Curtis was studying, and both were immediately welcomed back to time-in.

In the Nurtured Heart Approach, the table leg of relentlessly pursuing the positive is our over-arcing guide in all situations. In the first example, the student was progressively showing more positive choices. As the teacher remained focused on positives in the room, the student showed more and more self-control. Soon, there was total compliance and total success. This is the best possible option.

Yes, Bill could have been given a time-out for not going to his seat. At another level, though, if a teacher can avoid paying attention to a problem altogether, AND the student is taking steps toward solving that problem, a higher order of positivity is occurring. The student is totally managing himself rather than the teacher stepping in to manage him, and there is no interruption even for a second in the teacher's focus on reflecting success to the class.

Is it really that important to eliminate even a couple of seconds worth of attention to problems? YES! This is what we mean by *relentless* pursuit of the positive. The benefits are enormous. In this example, all the glory can go to Bill for redirecting himself.

In the second example, the teacher was, again, totally focused on the positive. In the room, Curtis was being double-dipped in positives, to no avail. When the teacher found Curtis still in the hall and went out to send him to the office, Curtis was already showing the behavior that was expected of him in the classroom. He was not saying, "Let me in and I'll be good." He was not making promises. He was ALREADY being successful.

Some students just have to know the teacher will not "lose it" no matter how hard they push; when they recognize this to be true, they suddenly stop pushing. Curtis had pushed and pushed Mrs. N. When she found him working in the hallway, he was completely "reset." She had a choice to go with that totally successful reset or impose her authority and administer the consequence (the referral to the office).

Everybody needs forgiveness and restoration. Curtis was literally crying out for it. He had already restored himself and wanted to be restored to the class. The student had essentially done a time-out (in the hall instead of the office), reset himself, and was totally ready for time-in. The teacher went with the positive in the moment. The forgiveness of the student was totally deserved by the student, and the teacher was asserting her authority by granting the forgiveness. Remember, YOU are the most valuable treasure in the room, and you are being incredibly powerful when you restore the student.

Wherever you find the positive—go for it!

**Not leaking negativity:** The teachers in these two examples were not throwing negative energy or extra time at the problem. They did not dwell on messy reminders, coaching, or warnings.

**Strictness:** In both instances, the teacher was being strict. In the first example, the rules were to come in and take a seat, and if you want to talk, raise your hand to be called upon. Mr. S waited for these rules to be followed before responding to the student. In that kind of circumstance, it makes sense to simply ignore the student's behavior until he gets it right. In the second example, Mrs. N was strict in that she kept on giving time-outs and eventually an office referral to a student who was massively disrupting the class. Mrs. N gave as many consequences as she needed to and then welcomed the student back only after he had totally redirected himself of his own accord. As long as these students were redirecting themselves in a positive direction, as long as they were improving, it made sense to keep ignoring them. Consequences would have been in order in the absence of signs of positive redirection.

Once in a while, the teacher can see that rule-breaking is going on but cannot tell who should receive the consequence. The temptation to stop class and do a little CSI (crime scene investigation) can be strong. Such was the situation in Ms. A's class when someone was humming during her lesson presentation at the board. When she turned around, the humming stopped. She gave the standard "don't you dare" glare and resumed, as did the hummer. After a few more such exchanges, Ms. A walked to the back of the class where the humming seemed to be coming from and asked, "Am I just going to have to teach from the back of the class today?!" No one responded, but she certainly left herself wide open for a clever remark. After a brief hand-on-hip silence, Ms. A went up front, reset herself, and began reflecting positives and appreciation to those who were focused, attentive, and contributing to the lesson. The humming resumed until two students turned around and told the hummer to knock it off. That was the end of the problem.

Keep referencing yourself back to those three legs. If you can't figure out whom to be strict with, keep pursuing the positive and don't leak negativity! Ms. A was certainly giving negative attention to the humming at first but got right back on track. Notice, however, that Ms. A did not leak further negativity by saying she appreciated those being respectful and quiet, which would have been a backward way of giving more attention to the hummer. It would have been signaling to the hummer that he was achieving negative relationship for the humming. If Ms. A had not leaked negativity from the beginning, she could indeed have praised the quiet, respectful behavior of other students; in other words, had she stayed positive throughout, the hummer would never have been engaged in a relationship with her over the problem.

Other situations may occur where students are throwing things, pestering each other, or accusing each other of doing things you did not see. Despite the temptation to launch a CSI, stand firm on the two table legs that you still have left: going for the positive and not leaking negativity. Do not surrender whatever legs you have left to stand on. The problem may go away; students may resolve it for you; or you may eventually catch whoever is involved. *Don't be in a hurry!* By pursuing the positive at every turn, you signal that the problem has no power over you. As long as you remain vigilant with the positives, you will probably come across the seeker of negative relationship fairly quickly. In the humming example, other students picked up the leg of strictness and then gave their peer what amounted to a time-out. Rather than deny or fuss, he accepted it. Time to celebrate!

## Their Behavior Is Their Decision
Here is a bit more on when to ignore and when to consequence, since this

question plagues many teachers. The guiding principle should be the student's behavior. If his behavior is improving, keep ignoring. If it keeps deteriorating, administer a consequence. This is very important because some students are adept at "appearing" to go into time-out/reset while actually causing as much confusion and frustration as possible. It might go something like this:

Teacher: "James, reset."

James says "OK" but does not reset and continues to act up.

Teacher: "James, are you going to reset or not!?"

James: "Yeah, I am –I just need this pencil."

Teacher: "James, I told you to reset and you need to reset."

James: "I am, I just need this pencil!"

James continues to say he is going to reset but is not doing so. The teacher gets frustrated and leaks more negative energy.

Here is a variation where the student has been reset, but at some point begins to subtly act as if he is not reset.

Teacher: "Ray, you are supposed to be reset. Are you ready to reset?"

Ray: "Yes."

Teacher: "You need to reset then."

Ray: "OK." However, the student continues to act as if he is not reset.

The key in both situations is that the student was not resetting and the teacher was getting into a discussion about the student's willingness or readiness to reset. Do not get into such discussions. Their behavior is their decision. James and Ray both decided not to reset. No discussion is needed, and any discussion would very likely be a leak. The best alternative is to just deliver whatever your school has decided will be the consequence for refusing a reset. The student may whine and wail that he was in reset, but ignore that. They will learn. The clearer the rules, the faster they learn.

## Setting Rules

Teachers often have questions about setting rules. Should it be done right away at the beginning of the year? If a student has done something "bad" but no official rule has been set forth about it, should their actions be overlooked until a subsequent infraction? Should there be rules about disrespect, or only behavior? Some teachers feel that if they have too many rules, the really "bad" students will be in time-out constantly, and nothing else will get done in class.

As stated in *Transforming the Difficult Child,* it is usually preferable not to set rules at all, and instead let experience (the praising of rules not broken, the praising of success, and the levying of time-outs) teach students what the rules are. In essence, the rules of school behavior have not changed in about 100 years, nor will they change much after kindergarten. Regulations about cell phones, weapons, drugs, and appropriate clothing happen at some point, but the basics never change.

Are the rules for players or fans of any sport posted near the court? No—everyone knows the rules after brief exposure to the game. Are we ever required to stop our cars on our way around town to review the rules of the road? No, because we are expected to know the rules and abide by them.

Instead of worrying about which rules and how they are conveyed, let us raise our expectations as high as possible: assume students know the rules of any classroom and of social interaction. Hold them to those rules. Expect that they will seek help if they get confused about them. It is quite common in the initial learning phase for students to ask why they were given a time-out. You are free to tell them after the time-out is served if they still want to know. *Do not tell them if they do not ask.* And the best way to tell them is in the context of praise in this new moment when they are not breaking that rule. Keep your expectations high, so students know you think they are capable of "playing the game" of life and school without reminders of any sort.

If you really want to have set rules—if you feel they are needed to really clarify what a student or classroom is to do, or you're starting the credit system to propel success (more on this in Chapter Seven)—then do so in a way that remains true to all three legs of the model. For example: In one very out-of-control classroom, the teacher made a rule that every student had to be in his or her seat at the bell, and no one could ask to get up until five minutes after the bell. These students needed to know the expectation in advance with total clarity. It would have been too protracted and difficult a process for students to "discover" that rule. At some point the rule will be unnecessary.

There are a few students who break rules at such a high rate that it is best to target them with only one or two rules until they are successful with those. With one very disruptive student, we began with only one rule: every time he got out of his seat, he was given a time-out. He quickly learned to stay seated. We then added time-outs for talking out. He soon learned to talk quietly and was less disruptive. Remember that, all through this process, the student is receiving vast numbers of positive recognitions. More rules can be added on as success increases. The rest of the class was held to all the rules, all the time. They never complained about the differential enforcement. We have found this to be the case in other classrooms as well. The main idea is for the teacher not to feel trapped by the rules.

Bottom line: If someone does something wrong, and it is not on the "official" list of rules, go ahead and give a consequence. Let common courtesy and common standards prevail.

## Attitude and Consequences

The disrespect shown by some students can be terribly invalidating. It's almost as if the teacher's very existence is nullified. Equally amazing to us is that some teachers respond to these challenges by trying to instill fear and/or humiliation in these students. It's practically impossible to want to behave for or truly respect anyone who is trying to embarrass you or make you afraid of them.

Attitude is like quicksand. Once you're in it, you're sinking. Struggle against it and sink faster. The idea is to never get in it at all. Thus, when we are asked if there should be rules about attitude, we generally say "No...not at first."

Can you really define something like rudeness, being a "smart aleck," being annoying, or sounding sarcastic? Rules need to be about behaviors, not attitudes. Stay in your seat? That's clear, that's measurable. Being sarcastic? Too many shades of gray there. Best to leave it alone. If you insist on giving consequences for displays of poor attitude, be prepared for lengthy arguments that spiral nowhere fast.

But there are some finer points that merit discussion here. Sometimes, you can wrap a rule around a display of bad attitude in a way that makes sense in the context of the Nurtured Heart Approach.

For example: If you give a student a reset and she says, "This is stupid" or "I hate you," you're best off ignoring these attitudes and focusing on whether or not she is doing the time-out. On the other hand, if the student blurts out "This is stupid!" in the middle of your classroom lesson, this is probably a rule violation (yelling out or interrupting); therefore, it should not be ignored but swiftly given a consequence.

The student must experience that her funky attitude cannot make you leak negative energy, yet she must also experience that you will always enforce the rules. If a student calls you a derogatory name, it is a rule violation, as every school has some rule about respecting the teacher. On the other hand, fussy and complaining attitudes are best ignored and not given any power. If, however, the complaining attitude crosses the line of arguing, and you have a no-arguing rule or any other rule that covers that territory, a time-out should be given.

A tone that is rude to your ears may be quite the norm in some households, neighborhoods, and cultures. For some children, their tone and bluster reflect a survival mechanism they've adopted to deal with tough circumstances. If you want it to sound better to your ears, just ask them to rephrase it. For example, it is quite common for some students to tell others to "shut up!" Just have the students "rephrase," which is like a verbal "reset." Soon, students can be overheard in the hallway telling others, "You need to rephrase that."

Remember that the main pathway for transforming students is your constant supply of praise and pursuit of their goodness and greatness. To do this, it is often necessary to ignore their attitudes and focus on their behavior. As they flop in the chair after being told to sit down, your response is something like, "That is real strength, Bill. To sit even though you are frustrated shows great strength." Do not fuss about or give a consequence for the flop. As they shuffle slow as molasses on their way to sit down, it's "Wow, Bill, you are on your way to your seat. That's real self-control." Remember, start with the rope at the bottom of the pool. You expect them to fly high someday, but this is where it starts.

Try to find success wherever you can in students' behavior and let attitude change on its own. This will happen as the students discover: (a) that their negative attitudes have no effect on you; and (b) that your relationship with them is all about reflecting their positive qualities, good intentions, and wise choices—your resolute faith in their value as a person.

## A Direct Hit

Every once in a while, a student will deliver a verbal blow to the heart of a teacher—an attack that lays bare something the teacher has struggled with for years or has hoped to keep hidden from public view. The teacher is shaken, hurt, and surprised that a student has been able to detect and then target whatever that sensitive thing might be. If this has not happened to you yet, we suggest that you prepare to respond to this moment with the following: "Your intuition and insight into people are amazing. That's a time-out." The broken rule was not being hurtful and a time-out needs to be issued. This response has incredible power. First of all, it shows that you are able to manage strong feelings without leaking negative relationship. Second, it takes the power out of the student's words by withholding from the student the ability to take your focus off the positive. Lastly, it takes the power out of the student's negative relationship with himself or herself. You have pointed out a gift and given a time-out/reset, after which the student can use that gift more wisely.

## For Very High-Rate Rule Breakers: Turbo Charging

Some students develop a pattern of seeking to frustrate you by always garnering time-outs. They break rules so fast that you can't keep up or give others the recognition they need—much less get to the lesson. Usually, these students are seen by their peers as very different from the rest of the class. These peers also generally accept that these difficult students will be held to a different set of standards than the ones to which they themselves are held.

You've probably noticed that the most difficult students are often ignored or shown occasional compassionate redirection by their peers. Rarely are such students rejected, ridiculed, or encouraged to act up by their classmates. Unfortunately, adults often are the ones to reject, ridicule, or encourage these problem students:

"You just need to get out of my classroom!"

"Are you crazy?"

"Keep that up and *see* what happens!"

Undeniably, such students are beyond frustrating, and successfully transforming them with this approach requires a major effort to avoid leaking negativity, which only lends energy to their acts of adversity. In fact, you'll have to find every possible reason to like the student who seems to want to destroy you. The good news is that these particular students are definitely after an intense relationship and thus ripe for this approach.

We have developed a specific two-part technique for these high-rate rule breakers—we call it *turbo charging*. As you begin this intervention, be sure to keep the rate of celebration fairly high for the rest of the class. This will prevent jealousy and clearly give the message that you are paying attention to everyone.

Turbo charging is an amped-up effort to give the difficult student every reason to see himself as competent, valuable, and likable. It is not a passive "wait, observe, then celebrate" approach, but involves even greater commitment to creating many opportunities for celebration. Do not ignore, tolerate, or pass the student off, but *go right at the student with your positive relationship*. Remember the pencil sharpener and meatloaf illustrations. Search every avenue to find ways to make this student competent and valuable as a person. Confront the child with his successfulness.

With high-rate rule breakers, you will want to be more "larcenous" in regard to stealing more of these positive moments. Turbo charging is about being more intense with the mirror you are holding up to reflect successes. Think of it as "the difference between hitchhiking and hijacking." **We are not just giving the student a ride into the positive; we are commandeering the whole process and taking that student hostage into successfulness** before he knows what's happening, with no chance of escape. We are not stealing some moments—we are stealing all of them! Think Shamu and toll taker.

Avoid treating this student as impaired, limited, compromised, or in need of management through special aides or additional manpower. Resolutely convey that the student is as important to you as anyone else, has meaning and positive influence in your classroom, and you enjoy him! Don't fear that the student will start acting up.

The two parts to this technique are: the specific enforcement of one or two rules to start with; and active engagement of the student that invites him to be totally successful in the classroom. Earlier in this chapter, under "Setting Rules," we explained how to enforce one or two rules as a starting point when dealing with high-rate rule breakers.

As for the second part of turbo charging, your goal is to create instances where the student can be successful even if it's not in academics per se. You might begin by asking the student for any ideas or reactions she might have to the lesson. "Jeanne, have you ever heard anything like the topic of the lesson?" "Does the topic remind you of anything?" "How do you imagine this topic might come up in your family?" "Do you agree or disagree with the way Joe [a classmate] sees this topic?" "Can you think of a word that rhymes with [insert topic-related word]?" Notice that none of these initial turbo charging questions requires any textbook knowledge.

The next phase is to begin asking more directly for textbook knowledge once you're sure the student can answer successfully. This can be done by cueing her about past successes: "Jeanne, you gave us a super answer last Tuesday that we need to hear again today. Could you help us all out?" Or, "Jeanne, you had this totally correct earlier in class. Would you repeat it for us again so everyone can get it right on the test tomorrow?" You might also use a cue for *future* success: "Jeanne, you have made some astounding inferences. What would you infer about this?" You will find that this strategy steadily increases the academic competence of the student. Continue to sprinkle in non-academic questions like those from the early stage of turbo charging so that you can help the student maintain a cushion of success and enjoyment.

Remember Pete, the student of Mr. Y whom we described earlier in this book? Pete was getting several detentions per day from teachers. He was a hilarious class clown, often suspended, and very hyper—and some days he was also terribly irritable. Recall that each morning, the staff members would be abuzz about whether Pete had taken his medication that day. If it seemed he hadn't, they would all brace themselves for battle. The negative energy toward Pete was evident even before he set foot in a classroom. Pete was treated quite differently on a day when he was perceived to be off his meds than when he was perceived to have taken them. Of course, Pete could sense his teachers' fear a mile away.

Teachers and administrators can spend considerable time telling Pete—and students like him—that they *must* learn and that they *must* behave. But this is futile when the student is only offered relationships that tell him he is bad, unwanted, and tolerated only until someone has had enough of him. He is told he will be a failure if he doesn't learn and behave, but he is *already treated as a failure, over and over* by the very process of people's negative expectations. As it is, people flinch when he walks into the room, or they look afraid, or they "get tough" right away, or they work hard to ignore him until they have reason to send him out. How is Pete to rise above this when people he is supposed to respect can't rise above it either?

Mr. Y was committed to going directly at Pete. He began by asking Pete questions several times each class period. Even when Pete said he didn't know the answer, Mr. Y would respond with something like, "I love your honesty, Pete. I bet other students are having a hard time with this lesson, too. Who has a question about molecules?" If Pete gave a completely wrong answer, Mr. Y would praise Pete's bravery: "An educated guess—that's science in action." Mr. Y was relentless. He wasn't letting Pete wriggle out of the viselike grip of his turbo-charged positive recognitions. In each 45-minute class period with Mr. Y, Pete was going to be successful, whether he wanted to or not. He was going to be helpful, informative, interesting, enjoyable, valuable, and—above all—he was going to BELONG, with as much to offer in contributions and participation as any other student.

After a week, Pete began raising his hand to venture a guess. He began to pay more attention, disturb others less, and do class work and homework. For the first quarter of the semester, Pete had been an F student and had done zero homework. About three weeks after the intervention began, he was up to a D+. Then he got a D, two Bs, and an A on quizzes—quite an amazing improvement, considering that he had been doing no work at all before. After about seven weeks, Pete was turning in 90 percent of the homework and had a C in the class.

When disruptive students like Pete begin to experience success, the rest of the class seems to dramatically improve as well—as long as the teacher has kept the rate of positives high for them, too.

Everyone in the class notices when this intervention is used. *The class sees the teacher making even the worst student a success, and this creates tremendous respect and safety for everyone.* It is even common for classmates to begin openly giving their support and encouragement to the formerly feared or ignored student. No child left behind, indeed!

## The Head Start Experience

By now you should realize that rewarding negativity is the problem with most conventional disciplinary approaches. With your own transformation firmly taking root, let's visit a preschool.

Walk into the door and watch those hard-working preschool teachers. When a little one breaks a rule, what do they do? Why, they redirect, of course! Redirection is probably the most cherished disciplinary tool in the preschool teacher's toolbox. After all, two-to-five year olds can't be expected to respond to a more rigorous version of discipline. They're too young. They don't have the self-control. Just take that energy that's going toward mayhem and funnel it into a new, non-rule-breaking activity. Easy as pie!

Hold on. Let's take a fresh look at redirection from the perspective of the child. I throw a block at my classmate and bonk her in the head...and what happens? A caring, gentle teacher comes right over to me! Wow! And she talks to me sweetly about how what I've done is wrong...and she then takes me over to a cool new activity and stays with me until I'm having fun with it. OK, I can play with the cars for a while, but after about five minutes, I'm getting bored again. How can I get that nice teacher to come and redirect me again? Oh, right—break a rule! I'll throw this car at someone.

See how it works? With redirection, we're still handing out energetic currency when negativity transpires. Preschoolers are no different than older children: they quickly see how effective rule-breaking is to grab adult relationship. And since they need lots of adult attention and don't have much internal self-control, these children stand to benefit hugely from energy handed to positivity. Short time-outs/resets work beautifully with very young children. Brief time-outs (15 to 20 seconds) followed immediately by a rich time-in work far better to reinforce good choices and remove energy from poor choices. Young children respond especially well to "reset" as a substitute for "time-out." One effective variation is "pause" soon followed by "play," or even "red light" and "green light."

A number of years ago, Howie Glasser gave a presentation on the Nurtured Heart Approach to a group of teachers and parents in Tucson, Arizona. A few attendees approached him afterward, telling him that they worked with the Head Start program—the preschool program for underprivileged and at-risk families whose children are more likely to face behavioral issues, diagnoses, and medication. They were interested in seeing whether this approach might help them with their particularly intense students. Howie was willing to try, but clearly stated that he would only work with all the students, not just their most difficult ones.

Head Start is known for its empirically based, formal, organized approaches, and they attacked this effort with this same attention to detail and pragmatism. Ten or so teachers and administrators proceeded to read *Transforming the Difficult Child* and learn as much as they could about the approach. They gave Howie packets filled with research and other materials Head Start had used as a foundation for its current approaches—which, incidentally, were not working to maintain order in quite a few of their classrooms. Not surprisingly, redirection was the main disciplinary technique used in the program.

The program embraced the idea that time-outs don't work and that they're bad for students. Head Start had tried to use time-outs in the past with poor results. This is no surprise, considering that they applied a "one minute per year" rule of time-outs: a four-year-old got a four-minute time-out, a five-year-old five minutes, and so on. Such long time-outs don't allow for a smooth transition to time-in. And good luck trying to get an extremely intense five-year-old to complete five minutes of time-out successfully! Short time-outs allow a quick transition back to positivity.

Following a lot of observation in the Head Start classrooms, Howie was asked to do a whole-class intervention with the Nurtured Heart Approach. Head Start staff watched the whole thing under a microscope. Within a week in each of 10 problematic classrooms, things had turned around. Often, it was the kids who had once been the worst-behaved who transformed into the best-behaved!

Even under heavy scrutiny from many observers, there was strong agreement that the non-challenging children were benefiting from the approach as well. The word "flourishing" was often part of the description. The benefit was so clear and undeniable that Head Start arranged a one-day training session with Howie for teachers from all 80 classrooms. Two thousand children stood to benefit. Head Start supervisors became expert in the approach and helped implement it throughout the Tucson Head Start system.

Before this all transpired, Tucson's Head Start had an entire mental health department to handle all the ADHD and other so-called mental health issues so common in its classrooms. The system also made many referrals out to the community for evaluation, diagnosis and treatment. Very costly endeavors! **In the first year the Nurtured Heart Approach was in effect in that network of preschools, there was not a single ADHD-related diagnosis.** For seven years, the success record has held: not a single child has been placed on meds for behavioral problems. An enormous amount of money was saved on mental health services, and the system was able to increase enrollment. At this writing, it serves about 3,000 children.

# Chapter Six

## *Famous Leaks*

THE NURTURED HEART APPROACH requires both limits and positivity. One or the other isn't enough. And those limits and positives need to occur at a level that matches the intensity of the child and the situation. When relationship and limits are clear and positive, students can relax and learn, and you can relax and teach.

Think of the limits and positives as two sides of a bucket, and the cool, clear water it holds as the child's inner wealth and capacity to learn. A negativity leak is like a hole in that bucket. And we all know that even when a hole is quite small, you can lose an awful lot of water before you manage to plug the leak.

We have referred to negativity leaks several times so far in the context of the three-legged table. What exactly is a leak of negativity? **A negativity leak is where the relentless pursuit of the positive is somehow undermined by negative expectations and/or by energy spent on problems.** It's quite easy to leak negativity without realizing it, especially as you are undergoing the transformation of mindset that is required to master this approach. Negativity can leak in very, very subtle ways.

Most of us are coming from places steeped in negativity—it's like background noise that we cease to hear because it's always been there. As has been discussed, nearly every approach to teaching and parenting under the sun proffers energized responses to adversity—for example, when "respect" isn't happening—in contrast to lower levels of energy and relationship when "respect" is happening. It's so prevalent that it becomes barely noticeable.

Much of the remainder of this chapter addresses what we refer to as "famous leaks" so that we can make you more aware of how to avoid them yourself and how to identify leaks in your own application of the approach.

This having been said, let's be clear on one point: **everybody leaks negativity** at some time or another. The goal is to refine the leaks from deluges to infrequent drips, to catch leaks when they're small, and to move yourself back toward relentless positivity. It isn't true that one must NEVER leak any negativity in order for this approach to work. That would be impossible.

## Nagging, Cajoling, Pleading and Constant Compliance

"You'd better not..."

"If you [fill in the blank], you'll get a disciplinary referral!!"

"I know what you're thinking of doing and you'd better wipe that thought right out of your mind!"

These are major leaks of negativity. The basic message to the student is, "I have a negative expectation of you and I dare you to confirm it."

Consider the expectation being conveyed when a teacher's aide walks into class, stands near a "problem child," and just stares at the student. The aide doesn't even have to look at the student. The fact that the aide chose to stand near the "problem child" is usually sufficient to convey the message. *Students will comply with your expectation!*

Early in his work with this approach, Tom Grove kept encountering specific problems that seemed beyond explanation. He decided to travel from class to class with students just to see what teachers were already doing. He saw that students who were absolutely hateful and defiant in one class were cooperative and contributing in the very next class. He saw that leaks of negativity with one student would suddenly give rise to widespread problems involving several other students: sometimes a class would go well for 40 minutes, and then a single leak of negativity from the teacher would result in turmoil. And why would a sudden burst of positivity toward even one student suddenly snap a classroom back into shape? Why were students so closely monitoring "fairness" via the number of consequences and "thank you" notes everyone had? As soon as there was any perceived unfairness, some students would cry out about it. (It should be noted that this isn't so much of a problem once a class is steeped in the Nurtured Heart Approach and the children feel a level of relaxing into their own inner wealth and a trust in being valued, but prior to that, unfairness can be the undoing of a classroom.)

The icing on the cake was this: One day, a teacher who excelled in use of the Nurtured Heart Approach was going to substitute in another room. It so happened that one student in that classroom was in that teacher's regular room and therefore had been exposed to the approach. She said to the teacher, "You're up in this room now, and that stuff you do won't work up here."

This incident helped cement Tom Grove's realization that *students are changing minute by minute based on the expectations being conveyed at any one time.* They are, in essence, instantly reflecting whatever the expectations are, positive or negative. *They are nearly always being compliant!*

We say "nearly" because students with very little inner wealth—or those with great amounts of inner wealth—have fairly stable internal expectations, which they are able to impose over the more variable expectations of others. Sporadic success has little impact on the pessimistic "I'm-no-good-and-never-will-be" expectations of those with little inner wealth. Sporadic failure will have little impact on the more optimistic "it's-bad-but-will-be-better" expectations of those with abundant inner wealth. Both become self-fulfilling as the internal expectations drive—even override—immediate external experience.

Between these two extremes are students who live in the moment, reacting to whatever expectations are being conveyed at that moment. As soon as positivity is conveyed, they act positively. These same students act negatively when the teacher leaks negative expectations. This explains how students can act very differently in different classrooms and environments. This also explains how one significant negative leak from a teacher can suddenly change the entire room. The negative leak changes the expectations in the room. Those students who are floating along, sensitive to whatever is expected, almost instantly comply.

The reverse happens when the teacher stops leaking energy on problems and starts conveying positive expectations via recognitions and praise. The students settle down and act more appropriately.

There is far more being communicated by you to your classroom than the words you choose. Expectations are also powerfully transmitted to others non-verbally by our demeanor. Your face, reactivity, gestures, voice tone, and posture are always telling others something about your inner thoughts and feelings. They may be positive or negative thoughts and feelings, but they will be signaled to others by the way you act—not just by the words you speak. Just consider the huge difference in your body language when you think "They'll like me," compared with thinking "They won't care." Students by and large are excellent at reading people's non-verbal, body-language expectations, readily putting two and two together. These expectations might be fleeting, but they are powerful. Below are some typical thoughts a teacher might have that could easily be conveyed to students in non-verbal messages.

- The class is about to get out of control. I can't handle this.
- Pete will be trouble because he hasn't had his meds today.
- It will be a good day if everyone can behave for only six more minutes.
- For a change (but probably not for long), Bill is finally acting as he should.
- All I am here for is to do my job and go home.
- These kids don't like me.
- They're ADHD—so what can I expect?
- This student is so useless/impaired by a tortured home life that she just can't be expected to behave.

These are the kind of reels that tend to run like background noise in teachers' minds. We may not even see that we're leaking negativity until we begin to think in the transformative, right-side-up manner of the Nurtured Heart Approach and realize how relentless positivity removes us from these kinds of negative expectations.

Negative expectations are all about fear...Fear that if you don't rein in students now, things are going to spiral out of control... Fear that if you can't get your students under control, you're not going to be able to shovel enough information into them to get them ready for testing... Fear that your students are out to get you... Fear of being judged by administrators, parents, or other teachers.

Negative expectations are overcome through relentless positivity about what is occurring in the moment and by letting go of negative expectations about the past or future. Fears dissolve when we stay in the moment. The Nurtured Heart Approach is designed to help you take fullest advantage of the present moment—the "now."

Expect your students to clearly know the rules and to understand that when you hand out a consequence, it's purely because the rules are just the rules, and the teacher's job is to enforce them, just like a referee in sports. It's no big deal; soon, students are back in the game. You expect success from them and they comply. Eventually, once they've experienced a few successes, students will expect them from themselves. That's how the Nurtured Heart Approach works.

Ms. H had an exceptionally impulsive new student who talked out, was often out of his seat, and was doing zero work. At Tom Grove's suggestion, Ms. H decided to time him out for leaving his seat and to praise him for any quiet, for any step toward doing work, and especially for raising his hand to speak. By the end of that class, he was starting some work and had begun to raise his hand. By the end of the week, he was following rules, working, and checking his own impulse to call out. He began doing better in other classes as well. What might have happened had they not scrupulously chosen to NOT give energy and relationship to his impulsivity?

## Consequences and Anticipated Behaviors

Sometimes teachers jump the gun and consequence a behavior that hasn't happened yet but seems likely in the context of the student's past behavior. This is a major leak of negativity that will send your three-legged table spinning to the floor. It is based in fear of what *might* happen, not in the actual happenings of the present moment.

One day, Ms. H entered the room and immediately gave time-outs to several students. Within a few minutes, she had given Cristan a detention. He was very upset and wanted to know what he'd done to deserve it. It turned out that she'd overheard Cristan talking about wanting to fight another student in the class. She did not want the students talking about fighting and worried that there would actually be a fight.

Fear was in motion and negativity was being leaked. Instead of giving a consequence for the breaking of a rule, Ms. H was doing it out of fear that a rule might be broken. Instead of operating out of fear, she could have openly celebrated how Cristan was *not* fighting. She could have found positives in his display of various abilities that made fighting unnecessary, or held up examples of his power over his strong emotions. He was still making wise choices despite his words, and he was creatively solving the problem of his anger by using words instead of fists.

Ms. A was excusing students to the computer lab one or two at a time as a reward for good behavior in her room. Emann had been quite talkative and was not being excused. He decided to get up and follow an excused student to the door of the room. Just before exiting the room, Emann stopped and asked, "Can I go, Ms. A?" She said "No." He returned to his seat and sat back down.

What's great is that Ms. A did not show the slightest fear that Emann would go out the door. All sorts of negativity could have been leaked in this situation. Ms. A could have yelled at him the second he'd risen from his seat, warning him not to go out the door or telling him to sit down. She could have told him, "Just for that, you'll be the last to go!" or added additional consequences aside from not being excused to the computer lab.

This last leak (adding on a punishment) is an important one. *The students were already in a consequence* because those not properly behaving were in a time-out from the lab. Emann was showing one of many possible behaviors demonstrating that he was not ready to go with his classmates. There was no need to add anything else to an already active time-out; his just continued. Fear is not only a major source of negativity leaks; it also can impede the enactment of strict, clean consequences. Ms. A neither leaked negativity nor added on a punishment for Emann. She could have taken it a step further, maximizing the positives in the situation: She could have praised Emann for stopping at the door. Instead of answering his question with a simple "no," she could have said, "You were acting wisely when you stopped yourself. What do you think you should do now?" Or, she could have waited for him to sit back down, then showered him with celebrations for such a wise choice—which really was the truth of the current moment.

Another teacher, Ms. K, is so fearless that she has put *nine* students in time-out at once on more than one occasion! She does it with complete conviction and without breaking stride in her offers of lavish positivity. Take a tip from her approach: *when you put students in time-out, you must not leak any doubt that they will do it.* Be patient; give the student a minute or two to make up her mind to do it. Jumping on students for not immediately doing the time-out leaks fear that they won't do it at all. Take a couple of breaths and trust that it will happen; and if it doesn't, you can administer a detention or whatever your school calls for when a time-out is refused.

Sometimes, certain students will be extremely vocal about how a teacher is picking on them, doesn't like them, and is out to get them. They get others involved: other students, parents, administrators. The teacher becomes fearful of giving any consequences to the student because complaints could fly, parents will call, administrators will intervene, and the school board might even jump in. This teacher may, in lieu of consequences, ignore major problems or issue many warnings or reminders to that student. In the student's eyes, this is experienced as yet more fussing and being picked on and as implicit permission to break the rules.

In an antagonistic, fear-soaked situation like this, the Nurtured Heart Approach has proven to be a blessing. Make sure your three-legged table is up and balanced, and it will withstand tremendous pressure. Make sure you pursue the positive with everyone involved, including parents and administrators. Be sure your rules are clear, based in behavior, and widely and consistently enforced. Make sure your rules are just rules so that you don't leak negativity by taking rule-breaking as a personal affront. Just as it takes time to build inner wealth and transform deep-seated negative expectations that some students hold, it will take repeated experiences to transform a situation like this.

Mr. Y had been carrying red "warning" cards around in his hand. When he needed a "thank you" note, he had to go to his desk to fetch one. We changed this around so that he carried the "thank you" notes and left the red warning cards on his desk. Carrying the warning cards instead of the praise notes was, in essence, a negativity leak. Students immediately noticed the difference!

"How can I be fearless in all this muck?" you might wonder. Our answer: *by knowing you can find positives in others who seem to be adversaries*—and by employing a process that is so obviously positive, in a way that can be easily seen by everyone involved. *When you feel fear or when things seem to be going poorly, pursue the positive all the harder.* Be strict, but not stern; be firm, but emotionally neutral. Students need to see that you can handle them and their intensity. Adults who confront you will most likely be startled, then disarmed, by positivity—after all, most of us are used to the opposite, particularly in a confrontation.

## The Wrong Consequence Can Leak Negativity

We cannot stop students from breaking the rules. We can, however, give them credit when they don't and consequences when they do. Giving a consequence or taking other actions to try to stop a student from breaking rules will leak negativity all over the place.

An example: Mr. P caught Sean playing with his Game Boy in class. He gave a time-out and requested that Sean hand over the game. Sean started arguing with Mr. P about whether or not he needed to give up the game in order to stop playing with it. When you think you need to take away the toy or game your student is caught playing with, and then argue that the student won't be able to leave it alone, you're plunging waist-deep into negativity. You are conveying to the student that he can't manage himself, when what really needs to happen is to fully give all of that responsibility to the student.

Think in terms of transformation. Think about how to confer maximum responsibility and maximum positivity to the student. Sean needs to learn how to resist temptation on his own and how to come up with coping strategies if he finds temptation to be a formidable foe.

As the teacher, one solution would be to time Sean out each and every time he breaks the rule. Let the student keep the object, but have him come up with a solution if he can't leave it alone. In either case, you are helping the student build his inner wealth. *Do not wait for the student to mess up!*

Praise the student's faith in himself to resist temptation—to turn himself around and to try to be more powerful than whatever is tempting him. Recognize him for keeping his word, for building trustworthiness, and for finding creative solutions to his problems. Even if the student ends up timed out again for playing with the object, you can praise his ability to successfully fight the toy's attraction for however many minutes he did so. You can use this kind of situation to make success the only option.

A couple of other real-life examples:

- In Mrs. H's room, two students were talking and being disruptive. Each got a time-out but they were allowed to continue to sit next to one another. She praised their cooperation and self-control. They finished class without incident.

- In Ms. P's room, two students were horse playing with one another. After their consequences were completed, the aide told one to move so they wouldn't be disruptive anymore. Both complained, and the student who was told to move made a big show on the way to his new spot in the room. Once there, he began pestering his new neighbor. Our recommendation would be to keep the students where they are and move rapidly into praising their new choice to *not* horse around.

## The Special Relationship

Vanessa had been challenging Mr. Y with disruptive behaviors for days. On this Monday morning, however, she volunteered to him that she had tried golfing for the first time over the weekend. Mr. Y jumped at the opportunity to bond with this difficult student and maybe forge a truce. They had a nice chat about golf but the next day, Vanessa was pushing the boundaries even harder than before.

Why hadn't anything changed? Most likely, Vanessa had been testing Mr. Y when she brought up the topic of golf. Sometimes, teachers feel that, if they can only strike up some sort of friendship with the student, they may be able to get along better. Mr. Y was trying to do just that.

We leak huge amounts of negative energy when we behave as though we have special powers or some sort of special relationship with students. We lose even more when we act like we *need* a special relationship. As teachers, a more beneficial and reliable aim is to help each student establish a special, powerful relationship with himself or herself. We do this by giving the student all the credit for her many successes and by giving her all the responsibility for managing her actions and emotions. Foster students' independence—not a special relationship.

Mr. Y could have "flipped" their conversation into a reflection of Vanessa's inner wealth. He could have remarked upon her bravery for attempting a sport as difficult as golf; for being a young female golfer in a male-dominated sport; or for being patient enough to take instruction from the person who took her golfing. This would probably have done a lot more for their relationship than an attempt to connect over a friendly conversation. By reflecting Vanessa's inner wealth, Mr. Y could have demonstrated that he didn't need anything from her; that he was there to celebrate and promote her relationship with herself; and that she was a joy in his eyes, no matter what. This would have established a boundary that she did not influence or control.

Life is hard when your ability to acquire, love, feel safe, and have fun depend on the whims and moods of people who have more power than you do. Many children are taught that this is the truth about being a kid—not because of any intentional teachings from parents and teachers, but because of the way more traditional parenting and teaching styles and schools of thought end up panning out. Children can end up feeling pretty powerless. When a child feels this way, is it any wonder that he seeks to drive your mood, or that he seeks revenge for unfairness? Is it any wonder he feels that appreciation of his essential self is unavailable and that he's willing to fight for whatever piece of the action he can get? People in general—of all ages—may feel so persecuted and miserable by others that they come to believe that the only way to feel powerful is to make someone else feel more miserable than they do.

Show these students that their real power lies in themselves and that you recognize it. Show them that appreciation is available and that they possess inner wealth. That's what this approach is about. If someone messes up, it's just "oops, broke a rule," reset and get on with time-in.

## Pausing the Class to Administer a Consequence

Mr. Y had a system of giving warning cards because of an administrative rule that students had to be given warnings before any consequence; two cards meant a detention. Mr. Y would walk silently to the student's desk, put the warning card on the desk, then look around at the whole classroom for a brief period before returning to the front of the class and getting back to the lesson.

Mr. Y was making some comments to build inner wealth, and he was being strict, but he was giving too much attention to problems when they occurred. A significant chunk of time and Mr. Y's energy were being focused on problem behavior. Because of the pause in the lesson, the entire class was also involved in the problem. He was leaking negativity. The class started having many problems; Mr. Y was puzzled and frustrated and soon found himself launching into a major lecture about rules. The problems increased, as did the energy and class time Mr. Y spent on problems and writing more and more office referrals. The solution was rather simple: Mr. Y shouldn't break stride at all when delivering a consequence and should keep pouring out the positives like water over Niagara Falls all the while.

## General Praise, Specific Consequences

Teachers sometimes leak negativity by giving general praise ("You all are showing great dedication!") while coupling it with very specific time-outs ("Jim, time-out"). In this case, the most direct, specific attention is being focused on problems, while success is being praised only in the broader context of the group. Students will generally go for the most specific attention, so problems usually increase in this situation.

## The Negative Effects of Positive Pep Talks

Ms. R's student, Michelle, was usually very inattentive, squirmy, and prone to outbursts of shrill laughter. Michelle's behavior improved when she had one-on-one attention, but this wasn't possible, so the next best thing seemed to be to separate her from other students. The student's desk was isolated in the classroom. Ms. R also gave Michelle her time-outs in the hallway. "I'm being really careful to not leak negativity—I've been giving Michelle a pep talk out in the hallway after each time-out, before she returns to class." (Again, we advise doing time-outs on the spot, within the classroom, when the rule is broken.)

A pep talk like the one Ms. R was giving leaks negativity in two ways. One is via process; the other is via content.

The process leak happens because the teacher is linking her hopeful, enthusiastic attention to the student out in the hallway. Any time Michelle needs some one-on-one attention, she knows the connection: rule-breaking will get it for her. Time-out for Michelle—and for her classmates who witness the whole drama—is a source of high doses of individualized teacher attention. Ms. R observed that Michelle was "very attentive, calm, and appropriate" during these pep talks—no small wonder, since she was getting exactly what she wanted. In turn, she was reinforcing Ms. R to do more of the same.

Ms. R was frustrated when Michelle would return to the room and cause more trouble right after displaying such calm, appropriate, attentive behavior. "When we talk, she seems like she really wants to try!" Ms. R said. But the big energy Michelle needed wasn't in the classroom—it was out in the hall, where they had their special talks and what Michelle perceived as special connection.

To better link teacher relationship and student success, Ms. R needed to keep Michelle in the classroom for the time-out and to celebrate her in the classroom context, the place where Michelle's successes need to be happening and appreciated. In fact, it would be best to move Michelle into—or very close to—the main body of students, where Ms. R could then fearlessly pursue moments of success. Then, Michelle's one-on-one connection with Ms. R can start happening in the classroom and with her peers. Notice that this involves Ms. R changing her expectations of Michelle and believing that she can make it as a regular student. How can Michelle make it as a regular student when she is separated in the room as a "special" student, or sent out to the hall? This is the mixed message some students get: "You should make it like the others, but you aren't like the others and have to be treated differently."

The content of Ms. R's pep talks also leaked negativity. Typical pep talks are along the lines of "You can do it, I know it"—an expression of the teacher's deep faith that the child can succeed if only she tries hard enough. Or, "You want to get through the rest of the class period without any more time-outs, don't you? I bet you can!" The unfortunate message that the child reads between the lines is: "But you are not doing what is expected now." And the well-intended pep-talk resonates in the child's bones as failure.

Some people respond well to pep talks from coaches or friends, drawing on that faith from another person as inspiration to jump back into the game more earnestly than ever. For students who are very difficult or have very little inner wealth, however, the outcome can be negative when the teacher predicts that the student will succeed—and the student fails.

To transform a child who believes she is no good and never will be, you need *credibility.* That means pursuing inner wealth as it is manifested in real time, linked to real evidence, rather than making predictions that may end up untrue. Present-moment evidence is as irrefutable as showing the child a photograph of what just transpired. It's hard to argue with a photograph. As you barrage the student with present-moment evidence of her successes, you build a foundation of credibility for yourself and a foundation of real successes for your student. More win-win.

Let the rules be the rules, and let the students' problems be their own problems. Expect them to manage their problems and give them all the responsibility to do so.

Sometimes, very young students just need to know some information about what to do and how to do it. Go ahead and give them the information they need. However, if you think they can figure it out, let them try. It will create a higher order of success for the student, because the success is all theirs. If you want to be peppy, be thrilled about their real successes and the inner wealth they reveal. That's the much more powerful version of a pep-talk. **Don't predict success; create it right then and there!** Everyone will have something to be happy about.

## More on Process Leaks

By *process,* we refer to sequences of events—the way things are being connected. Take, for example, the process where student negativity leads to a teacher praising and celebrating, but then quitting when the class shapes up. Students then act up again. The teacher celebrates, but backs off again; and, after a period of good behavior, students erupt. This is a process—a sequence of events—marked by student negativity, which then results in temporary positivity from the teacher.

How will students get more positives? Act up. To avoid this slippery slope, you have to keep one eye on the process and the other on teaching.

A process problem typically occurs when you feel you are doing what you need to be doing, but for some reason it isn't working. When this happens, check to see if one or more of the following feels true:

1. Am I afraid?
2. Am I taking long pauses, wondering what's going on?
3. Am I thinking and talking about nothing but lesson to the exclusion of building inner wealth?
4. Am I hoping class will be over soon?
5. Am I feeling resentful and underappreciated?
6. Am I using the approach only in *reaction* to the students?
7. Am I thinking that the students have forgotten the rules?

If you are reacting to the students (#6), you will soon be doing #2 (wondering what is going on)—and, probably in close succession, #4 and #5. You think you are being positive and enforcing rules, and you probably are; the problem is that *you have not taken full charge of the room.* You start thinking along the lines of "Hey, I've been real positive, they should be good for a while," or "Can't they be good for just five more minutes while I get attendance done?" This amounts to leaking negativity as you try to tread water. You are surrendering your mood to the students.

Luckily, the solution to all of these problems is the same!

First, think **"total domination by positivity,"** and manifest this as though your life depended on it. Second, calmly and coolly enforce rules. Third, repeat one and two over and over. Quickly get your three-legged table back up!

Ms. H was frustrated. Her class was holding it together, but there was plenty of room for improvement. Many students were working on their labs, yet they were noisy, grouchy, and wandering around too much. She was praising, but only when turmoil was happening. She was clearly hoping the class wouldn't erupt before they made it to clean-up time. The mood of the room was not fully in her hands. Suddenly, she started broadcasting lavish praises. She kept going, and within minutes the class was settled, calm, and relaxed. So was she. She then poured it on some more until the bell rang. No time-outs were needed. She was bringing the children along in their ever-deepening inner sense of being valued and of being capable of making wise choices.

Ms. L had a new class of sixth graders coming in. They entered the room with much fussing, taunting, and hollering. Once inside, they continued to wander around the room. Ms. L welcomed and praised the students and quickly put four students in time-out. She never lost her pace of celebration, continuing to offer smiles and warm welcomes. The time-outs were over in less than a minute. As she was learning names, she put three other students in time-out. Her three-legged table was standing and strong: she was relentlessly positive, not leaking any negativity in her actions or words, and strictly enforcing rules. The class settled down and was ready to go in less than seven minutes from the initial bell. No more rules were broken and plenty of smiles were seen throughout the rest of the class period. Later in the term, she received high compliments from two students who told her that she was "the nicest mean teacher they ever had!"

## Pushing the Lesson

This is a very common process problem and a difficult one to avoid.

Many teachers are taught that the best class management technique is a good lesson. That is rarely true in our experience. We often see fabulous lessons completely ignored and scorned because the students are so driven to have some relationship going on. They are starving, and a lesson is not the nourishment they seek. When you push the lesson instead of the "hidden curriculum" (the social curriculum), students immediately perceive that the lesson supercedes them in importance. Disruption follows. Given all the pressure put on teachers to follow a curriculum and document that they taught this material this day, teachers have a lot of fear about holding back from shoving the lesson through the din of disruption. The teacher will be blamed for any poor achievement and may have to reteach the material.

Thus, most teachers have all sorts of anxiety when we advise them to teach inner wealth first and the lesson last. *Students must first experience that the flow of inner wealth is not just a trick, but a constant, sincere way of life.*

A telltale sign that students detect is when a teacher finishes a blast of inner wealth, looks around the class, sees that it has settled down, then says, "OK"— probably without even realizing it—and jumps into the lesson. That "OK" sends the message: "I got what I wanted, so now I can do what I really want to do." The teacher just wanted the students to behave. This usually leads to rebellion and further delays in getting to the lesson.

Voice energy plays a role in the process leak. Teachers often talk very loudly when teaching their subject to make sure everyone hears the lesson. Many teachers preface important elements of the lesson by saying "this is important" or "this is crucial" to help ensure that no student misses what comes next. Some teachers get even louder when problems come up. The end result is that the energy given to praise and recognitions of inner wealth pales in comparison. Again, students perceive the lesson and/or problem behavior as more important, even if the rate of praise has been high.

Tom Grove has helped several teachers turn this upside-down hierarchy of vocal energy right-side up by using the loudest voice for inner wealth, a conversational level for the lesson, and a very flat conversational voice for time-out. This works incredibly well! Students begin to perceive the inner wealth as very important. They get very quiet to hear the lesson. Time-outs abound, but so do recognitions of success. Once this change has been locked into place, any student who tries to talk while the teacher is teaching sticks out like a sore thumb. Soon, the room is functioning smoothly; the need for time-outs diminishes; and inner wealth is so clearly the main lesson.

To stop pushing the lesson with vocal energy—to make it secondary to the joy of teaching inner wealth—requires a huge shift for most teachers. However, when they do it, their teaching time expands, the students want to learn, and achievement takes a jump. By pursuing the learner, you teach a lesson more valuable than any textbook contains: *You are important as a person, first and foremost. In fact, you are downright wonderful! By the way, here is some math that might interest you.*

## The Dangerous Business of Archeology

Sometimes students' actions seem to defy reason. We want to know why they did what they did. We begin to dig through the rubble. This is, as the section heading clearly states, dangerous business.

Students, especially teenagers, are experts at obfuscation. We dig, they shift like sand, and the scenario ends in confusion and frustration. Many students don't really know why they do things and offer excuses or outright lies to appease us. They reinforce their position as "problem children" when they take this route.

Asking "why" is like mining for problems—mining for negativity. The question "why" usually leads us to the existence of a problem or an unacceptable behavior. For the child who already has come to believe that she receives more energy and relationship through adversity, the mere discussion can reinforce that belief.

In its purest form, the Nurtured Heart Approach does not need to know why. The student's past or even the student's motivation for present behavior is irrelevant because our overriding goal is to create inner wealth in the same manner for every student. We praise steps toward positive coping, give consequences for rule breaking, and hold the student responsible for solving the problem. We want to create situations where success is the only option.

If you do ask why a student has done something negative, make sure to convey that it will not hurt the student in any way for you to know the answer. Avoid all overtones that the student is bad or "being stupid," that the student is a "poor victim" whom you are trying to rescue, or that the student is "hurting" you.

If you do ask, ask only *once*, and don't push for the "real" reason. Show the student that you trust the answer you got. Ask as a scientist, or as if you believe the student has a good reason. If you ask a straight question and get a straight answer, you can praise the intention or character of the student. This could turn into an opportunity for the student to do some problem solving.

At one school, Tom Grove was asked by an assistant principal to help with Tony, a chronically difficult student. Tony had just thrown his loaded book bag clear across the room at the teacher, missing her by a foot. In the office, Tom found Tony slumped dejectedly in a chair, weathering a strident administrative lecture.

"Why did you throw your bag at your teacher?" Tom asked Tony.

"I was mad," Tony replied. "She promised to call on me. For two days I've been waiting, and she still didn't call on me!"

Tom took this opportunity to praise Tony's desire to participate in class and to be noticed by his teacher. He also praised Tony for studying so that he was prepared to be called on and for having the patience to wait two days. Of course, Tony was given a consequence for his choice of tossing the book bag. However, his initial intentions and desires were wonderful and valuable. A straight question was asked and a straight answer given. If he had responded with anything else, the pursuit of "why" would have ended, and the focus would have turned to searching for positives the student was exhibiting in the moment.

Brian had stolen for the third time in three weeks at school and was being suspended for eight days. His parents watched as an administrator reamed their son out. They waited until the school finished doing its business then turned to their son and praised how he had looked the administrator in the eye, made no excuses, accepted responsibility, and sat patiently. They then expressed their hopes that he would figure out how to stop stealing soon.

That was all they needed to do. These parents had driven themselves nuts trying to find a good reason for Brian's behavior, asking him again and again why he stole. He never gave a straight answer to their inquisitions. When they shifted to the Nurtured Heart Approach, they recognized that they could hold their child responsible for his actions and for solving his problems.

Sometimes, venturing a "why" can produce an opportunity to praise and can lead to opportunities for problem solving for the student, but in general it is unwise. If you want to become an archeologist—if you want to ask why—be careful to avoid feeding negative relationship when you ask, and be sure you can ask once and quit.

## More Famous Leaks

- "You are doing great, but you need to raise your hand/work quietly/stay in your seat."

This says to the student that she is really *not* doing great, as mistakes or un-wanted qualities are still present. It's like saying, "Here is a cookie, but it doesn't taste great" or "Yes, I really love you…but you could use better table manners next time, OK?" Does this sound like positive recognition?

- "Why, even Beth is working today!"

  Beth usually does no work in class and everyone knows it. Today, she does some work, and it's cast as a near-miracle. Beth is actually singled out for embarrassment by this type of comment, and it further energizes her "his-tory" of negativity instead of focusing on the success of the moment.

- Stern looks…

  This is a non-verbal leak, and probably the most frequent leak on the planet. The teacher is trying to stop something bad from happening by giving that "don't you *dare*" look. Remember: this is actually an advertisement to stu-dents that you have a button they can push. It signals to the student that you have an investment in the rules—that the rules are part of your rela-tionship with the class rather than just rules. Lastly, it implies that you can stop students from breaking rules—which we maintain you cannot. If they want to break a rule, they will.

- "*You're-great!*" (Said faster than a speeding bullet…)

  This is usually insincere and perfunctory, often done by hurried teachers.

- "Carl has HIS book out."

  While this teacher is looking to be positive about who has their books out, the undertone represents a slam against anyone who doesn't. It also is not a positive recognition of Carl.

- "Come on everyone, there's only six more minutes of class left."

  The class has gone well, the teacher has backed off the rate of positive recog-nitions, and she's hoping—in this case, pleading—that the class can coast the final few minutes without falling apart and acting up. This is not a praise nor a consequence; it is a leak.

- "That's a reset!" (Said sternly and accusatorily)

  This is clearly a reminder and a threat, and even more: a clear signal that the student is under the teacher's skin. It leaks negativity.

- "I'm sorry, but you broke a rule and I have to give you a detention."

  This implies that the teacher is trying to be the student's "pal" and will suffer from the child's consequence right along with the child. But remember: the rules are just the rules. There is no need to apologize or feel bad about giving a consequence. There is no need to make this part of the relationship. Just reset and get ready for time-in.

- "Next time, ask or you'll get a time-out."

  Rather than a clean consequence, the student gets a warning and a reminder of what to do next time. Essentially, the teacher is ignoring the rule and also leaking negativity. This is another subtle yet important way that personal relationship can be wormed into rule enforcement—to everyone's detriment.

- "Jimmy, can YOU answer this one?"

  Here, the teacher is trying to get the most problematic/underachieving student to answer the simplest question, but her unspoken expectations (doubt that the student can manage it) are apparent in the teacher's voice and posture. This leak of negativity almost always leads to a problematic student acting even more so! We cannot stress enough the importance of having positive expectations, and high ones at that. Our low expectations leak out even when we try to cover them up with nice words. The good news is that, as you expand your adventure of building inner wealth, high expectations will be a natural outgrowth of all the new positive choices you witness and celebrate.

- Patting a student on the back as you give him a time-out.

  The teacher is generating confusion in the form of some positive relationship mixed with rule enforcement. If I want another pat on the back, I should act up. If I don't like it, I can tell the teacher "Don't touch me!" and get some negative relationship with a large helping of the teacher's energy on the side.

- Lowering your standards and expectations for certain "special" students on an ongoing basis.

  One effect of lowering standards and expectations for certain students: the classroom begins to believe that the rules are not the rules for everyone. The other effect is that the student accorded this "special" treatment will not rise above what you expect. If you think the student cannot learn to sit in her seat, she won't. If you think a student has such a bad family that he needs special considerations, you are handicapping him by not treating him as fully part of a wonderful regular school family. You've probably heard the saying,

"Argue for your limitations and, for sure, they're yours." Similarly, arguing for others' limitations, even subconsciously or with body language, will help make their perceived limitations all the more real.

- "Now, this is what a class of 8th graders should look like. This is great!"

  While this sounds positive, it reduces all the students to an amorphous group and implies that all you really wanted was a well-behaved crowd—especially if you follow it with pushing the lesson. Students need and deserve specific recognitions.

- Allowing time to lapse between the breaking of a rule and the levying of a consequence.

  During the beginning stages of enacting the Nurtured Heart Approach, it is essential to closely link the rule being broken and the consequence. One reason is so the student can make the clear connection. Another reason is so the student has no time to argue with you about what happened. Once everyone sees that you are simply enforcing rules and REALLY creating a super time-in, you can delay enforcing rules when it is more convenient to do so.

# Chapter Seven

## *The Credit System*

*Credit systems aren't necessary in the Nurtured Heart Approach. In other words, they aren't required for the Nurtured Heart Approach to work.*

IF YOU DECIDE THAT A SYSTEM OF REWARDS MIGHT SUIT YOUR CLASSROOM, please keep in mind that we in no way want to suggest a major undertaking that will create yet another time crunch in your day. However, should you decide to implement a credit system, it needs to be part and parcel of the Nurtured Heart Approach and not at cross-purposes. You can feel free to sculpt and streamline the principles presented here to meet your needs. Many teachers already have credit systems up and running; your system may require a few minor tweaks in order to work in greatest harmony with the Nurtured Heart Approach.

Some children need very concrete objects, like points and an exchange of privileges, to help them bridge into the joy of relationships. The "stuff" captivates these children until they are at the point of experiencing their inner wealth growing. As you will see, the greatest opportunity for earning points in this approach comes from showing pro-social behavior—not in exchange for chores or tasks common to most incentive systems. The credit system in this approach simply distills down to being a device to propel inner wealth. It is a vehicle to deliver powerful positive statements of acknowledgment.

It could be said that we are *all* on credit systems. In early childhood, we recognize that we can earn some of life's pleasures through good choices, performance of chores, or achievement in school. Later on, we work for money, which is just another version of the credit system. In the real world, the amount of work doesn't always translate into an equal amount of financial award (particularly in education!), but we can create a credit system "economy" for our students that feels fair and that amplifies their understanding that the rewards for following rules outweigh the rewards of negativity. Using a credit system helps us codify those privileges so that children can consciously choose how to use the good "mojo" they receive not only for following the rules, but for being a super citizen in school. They can look forward to spending their points just as you can look forward to spending your hard-earned money on something you really want or need.

A well-thought-out credit system teaches children about economics well before they are thrust into the earn-and-spend world as young adults. They will have had the experience of being in charge of an economy, budgeting and spending points with forethought. Probably, they will have made some mistakes with their points, which in turn will help give them a foundation for their financial know-how as adults.

For difficult children, the credit system is particularly advantageous. They have learned that the way to acquire things they want is through begging, stealing, bullying, class-clowning, passivity, or manipulation, not through dedicated earning and careful spending. Difficult children often find that their ability to acquire the things or privileges that they want hinges more on the whims and moods of their parents than on their own behaviors. Some of these children find it all too easy to get whatever they want from their parents, regardless of poor behaviors, as their parents make repeated desperate attempts to attain closeness, leverage, or gratitude. Or, the parent might allow unearned privileges like more video game, TV or computer time just to have some blessed relief.

The credit system helps clarify the classroom's economy so that it is congruent with expectations. It diminishes the need to "extract" attention or privileges from adults.

For the teacher, a credit system offers a systematic way of acknowledging and encouraging every one of your students. It creates an economy that can help you appreciate and give credit for "micro" efforts that, together, add up to the big picture of student success. It provides strong support for rule enforcement in your classroom. The message to students is, "I can't stop you from breaking a rule, but I can give you recognition and credit when you make the choice *not* to break the rules and a consequence every time you break one." The credit system can help show children that rules are not the enemy—that, in fact, more rules are better! Students can feel they are doing their job of following the rules with tangible benefits.

Most parents and teachers of difficult children are already using bits and pieces of credit systems in their attempts to gain leverage, but these bits and pieces are informal, unpredictable, and disorganized.

"If you eat your broccoli, you can have some dessert."

"If you have a good week at school, you can sleep over at Joey's on Friday."

It's a dangle-the-carrot, manipulative tactic, not an economy—as though someone walked up to you on the street and said, "Hey, if you do this odd-job for me, I'll give you 25 bucks." You might go for it once, but this kind of random earning strategy is not going to provide any foundation for you long-term. Still, this kind of bargaining may work just fine with some kids. But difficult children—the ones who can turn a classroom upside down in the blink of an eye—benefit from a much more structured and predictable credit system.

A credit system helps you maintain neutrality instead of being pulled into negativity. Your decisions about what to reward and what privileges to offer students are not arbitrary or based on your emotional whims that day; there's a bottom line of points earned and available for spending. You—and the world at large—end up being seen as more fair, consistent, and predictable.

## How to Design A Credit System for Your Classroom

First, be sure your rules are in place. Remember that rules should be totally clear and stated in the negative so there is no "wiggle room" between following the rule and breaking it: "No back talk," "No bad words," "No yelling," "No name calling." Include a few "gimme" rules that children will almost always follow consistently so that you always have the option to recognize students for not breaking a rule. Set the system up for success as well as leverage. For example, you can award points to students for walking away from a conflict with another student instead of getting into an argument or fight.

You can post rules somewhere in your room, or if you know that your students know them—and they should, if you've been recognizing students for following them—move on to the next step.

Next, formalize a list of desirable, sought-after behaviors and qualities. This is your **Ways to Earn** list. You can refer back to the characteristics of inner wealth in Chapter Four for some ideas, or the list of values in Chapter Three. Good attitude, extra effort, being respectful, using good manners, showing responsibility, helping to clean up, making a good choice, taking "no" for an answer, helping the teacher, following directions, cooperating, and sharing are a few examples. Write this list down, because you will be tracking and crediting the qualities on that list. In other words, you will be awarding credits and bonuses both for rules not broken and for positive behaviors and efforts applied to responsibilities. Break your Ways to Earn qualities down into several specific components so that you have plenty to reward and celebrate. Remember the pencil sharpener and the meatloaf!

Next is your **Ways to Spend** list. This list consists of privileges you find acceptable for your students, which they can earn through constructive behavior.

In this system, points are given generously to students to enhance the verbalized version of acknowledging each success. **Points are never taken away.** They are only used to purchase privileges. **The only ways to miss out on future privilege are:**

- **Not accumulating the necessary credits**

- **Refusing to fulfill a consequence**

The student is unable to spend points while he is having a problem or not finished with a consequence or class work.

Points can be spent in a variety of ways on special activities, privileges, or even a "get out of time-out free." These pages provide a list of suggested privileges that we have seen used successfully in schools.

Try to offer students a rich array of choices. You can be as entertaining and

## Classroom Privilege Ideas

Computer time

Pencils, stickers, erasers, or other small gifts

Choosing an activity

Choosing a story for the class

Weighing or measuring items

Learning a magic trick

Teacher's helper

Giving a spelling test

Talk with a friend

Assist custodian

Use typewriter

Be a peer tutor

Special reading time

Choosing the sport at recess

Mentoring in a lower grade

Eraser cleaner

Correct papers

Time with art materials

Messenger

Visit with previous year's teacher

Special visit with the principal

Helping to decorate

Record a story

Watering the plants

Helping in the cafeteria

Homework excuse passes

Hall monitor privilege

Good report home via phone or note

Praise note to principal

Cruise the classroom offering praise to other students

creative as you feel inspired to be. One ingenious parent even allowed her foster son to use points to "buy" an argument and was subsequently able to applaud the thoughtful points he made during his earned argument. Be generous, and don't hesitate to make a privilege that has always been offered "gratis" into a privilege that is purchased with credits.

If you already have a credit system in your classroom, you know how it works: **If a student follows a rule, shows an example of good behavior, or performs a chore or responsibility, he is entitled to earn the corresponding credits.**

The difference between most credit systems and the one used with the Nurtured Heart Approach is that the latter is extremely generous: it gives points freely and never takes them away. If you apply the basic approach diligently—that is, use all the phases of recognition to build inner wealth—you can achieve just as much with a credit system that is generous and positive. You are empowered to keep the credits flowing as you reward success and bestow recognition rather than using the credit system in a negative, punitive manner.

This kind of credit system allows difficult children to apply their intensity toward privileges instead of toward trouble. It can really bring about a strong transformation in these children. The credits are a tangible representation of appreciation and success. *The credits, however, are never simply given in the absence of the verbal recognition.* The credit system can become a superb reminder to the adult to give recognition, even on stressful days when one might otherwise forget.

Since you are using the credit system for multiple children, you may benefit from the use of actual "markers" handed out to students, like currency. We've seen parents use poker chips, play money, and homemade tokens or tickets. This gives the child the added responsibility of holding onto those markers until she is ready to spend them. The accounting becomes quite easy when you use actual credit currency instead of a chart with stickers or other markings. You needn't worry about keeping track of credits earned; all you need to do is hand them out and collect them as they are spent. And there's an added benefit: with markers of different denominations, you can teach a lot of math through the credit system!

## Generosity, Generosity, Generosity!

Make point values high. Why give one point for a success when you can give 10? High point values also make it easier for you to give partial credit for increments of success. Here's one place where inflation is a *good* thing.

You can assign higher credit values to behaviors or achievements that are more important to you. Offering higher credit values for success in especially difficult areas can help stack the deck for faster transformation; but if you need to have all credit values the same—which you probably will, due to time constraints—the system should still work for you.

For example: For homework, you could assign 10 points each to different aspects of completion. This teaches children the wonderful life lesson that the *process* of achieving a result is important and worthy of recognition. They are less likely to be overwhelmed by the pressures of achieving that result because they know that recognition is available at many points along the way.

The more you break down tasks into smaller components, the more successful younger students or easily-frustrated students will be. Your expectations are precise and you have all kinds of opportunities to reward success.

Another way to be generous is to give bonus points for such qualities as displays of compassion toward one's self or others; taking criticism well; apologizing when appropriate; or doing something thoughtful for another student. Feel free to invent whatever bonus credit feels right to you, and feel free to experiment and change direction as needed. And you can have "red apple days" where privileges are half-price or even days when they're given away for free.

## Partial Credit

You can keep successes flowing by granting partial credit for incremental steps toward total success. For example:

"Anthony, I am going to award you half of the usual 10 points today for following the no-hitting rule. You controlled your hitting for most of the day today. Great self-control."

Recognizing these small successes helps your students realize that they do not have to be perfect to be valued in your eyes and it gives you the vantage point of discerning a greater degree of the actual truth of the moment. For a child who broke a rule once during the day, the truth really is that most of the day was a victory in choice and control over not breaking that rule the rest of the day.

## Get the Parents Involved

Really, the best place for a difficult child to have a credit system is in the home. His parents are much more able to institute a credit system that perfectly suits their child. If parents seem open to instituting a credit system for a child whose behavior is challenging in school, their best resource is the first book on the Nurtured Heart Approach, *Transforming the Difficult Child*. That book will show them how to design a credit system in the home that will make success even more unavoidable for their child!

The very best way to introduce this approach to a parent, however, is to wait until you are seeing the impact of your inner wealth efforts in the classroom and then contact the parents to congratulate their child. Instead of calling them about problems with the child, you are opening a doorway to tell them what you believe their child is responding to and to share key concepts about the approach. Our experience is that the parent will be much more likely to be receptive to what you have to share under these positive circumstances.

We want to emphasize that, while a credit system can have a wonderful, fun influence in your classroom, it certainly is not a requirement of this approach. If you decide it can work for you, streamline it to whatever extent necessary to make it comfortable and easy. Create it in a way that works for you. It is simply a vehicle whereby children can trust that their successes will be seen and noted on a daily basis.

# Chapter Eight

## The Whole School Orchestra:
## Have Your Principal Read This Chapter

WE HAVE SEEN NOTICEABLE BENEFITS accrue in schools in which one or more class-rooms institute the Nurtured Heart Approach. Overall, students and teachers benefit even when this shift is made on a small scale. But the benefits seem to multiply exponentially when school administrators find a way to ordain a school-wide implementation. When all is said and done, the most crucial step toward the optimal well-being of every child in the school building is that of applying this approach school-wide.

Undoubtedly, the decision to mandate a specific approach is a difficult one for any administrator. A principal who is considering doing so must weigh all options and measure all pressures. Principals also must factor in relevant issues and points of view voiced or held by the district, school board and teacher's union.

Some principals consider all these issues and end up feeling that they would be stepping on too many toes if they mandate the use of this approach school-wide. Many administrators who have studied educational leadership come to believe that all decisions that affect school faculty should be made by committee, using a democratic process. Many fear the adversity that might arise if they were to make an autocratic decision. Some feel more comfortable starting out slowly and experimentally, with a few classrooms; once they find that the approach works, they hope and pray that interest will spread to the other classrooms by some osmotic process. Or they hope that a few classrooms will produce data compelling enough to influence others who stand to benefit from the approach.

More empirically-minded principals and administrators want solid research on which to base a decision as radical as implementing a school-wide approach to discipline. This is certainly understandable. The stakes are high. Many so-called "blue-ribbon" programs are backed by reams of empirical data, but many disappointed leaders have found that—voluminous research notwithstanding—the program is too hard to use, not replicable in their classrooms, or just doesn't yield the desired changes. In our experience, this outcome is quite common. And many of these programs come with a hefty financial price tag.

As a result of all of these concerns and differing viewpoints on the part of administrators and principals, it's difficult to convince most that the whole-school implementation of the Nurtured Heart Approach is well worth a try. All we can say here is that those administrators who actually step up and make an autocratic call on behalf of all of their students are the ones who seem to wind up way ahead of a game that could otherwise be maddening. These few courageous exceptions to the rule have shown us that a whole-school Nurtured Heart application is a winning solution for everyone involved. If the children win, then so do the teachers, the parents, and the community. Everyone wins.

Those administrators who are exceptions are worth our study. They are the people who are breaking new ground. They can show us whether a new way of doing things is ultimately awful or wonderful. The history of every discipline is full of accounts of innovators who were told they couldn't possibly...they shouldn't dare...it would be too big a risk...it will never work. And lo and behold, they turn out to have been onto something spectacular all along.

Case in point: Maria Figueroa, principal of Tolson Elementary in Tucson, Arizona. In the days following a two-hour in-service primer on the Nurtured Heart Approach at Tolson, she visited classrooms and observed carefully. She found that some teachers made some changes based on the approach and observed clear benefit. She saw that some teachers made no changes and noticed the same old problematic behaviors. And she noticed that some teachers made significant changes, abandoning prior methods that weren't working and wholeheartedly adopting this new approach. In those classrooms, she saw tremendous benefit.

What Mrs. Figueroa did next was stunning and daring. Ultimately, her decision won her acclaim, and rightly so. She went to the next faculty meeting with a plan.

She started by applauding all the teachers who had made changes beneficial to the children of the school. She then announced that, on the basis of what had transpired since the in-service, from now on Tolson was "Nurtured Heart—all the way." She offered support, encouragement and mentoring to anyone wanting to get on board. Then she told her staff: "If you choose not to use the approach, that's okay. But it's only fair for you to know in advance that from now on, evaluations will be heavily based on how well this approach is put into action. Anyone who is sure they don't want to use this approach might want to reconsider to avoid a poor evaluation. Or, you may want to find another school where you can do as you wish."

Within a month, virtually everyone was on board. The rest is history: dramatic shifts from low to high test scores; from high use of special education services to extraordinarily low use; from high teacher attrition to low; from high rates of diagnosis and medications to almost none;[9] and from high rates of student suspensions and bullying to almost none.[10]

---

9. No child has been recommended for medication by the school, but in a couple of instances parents have turned to medications in an effort to help their children.

10. In his last conversation with Mrs. Figueroa before this book went to press, Howie Glasser was told that one child was suspended twice for bullying. The school had made huge progress with him, then he relocated to another school.

Administrators who decide to exercise their quiet power are desperately needed in today's educational system. These leaders really step up and take bold action, trusting their guidance and inspiration rather than playing it safe.

Is your principal ready for some bold action? Read this chapter first, then show it to your principal. Encourage him or her to read the entire book and to observe your use of the approach in your classroom.

## The Music of the Social Curriculum

Most schools give license to teachers to do their own thing in conducting a classroom. It sounds so compassionate and logical. But because of this laissez-faire practice, too many schools end up the equivalent of a cacophonous orchestra—an orchestra that we would have difficulty listening to.

Think about it: a school building comprised of 30 teachers using a variety of different teaching methods, disciplinary methods, and social curriculums. On top of that, the administrators often have their own varying ways of dealing with student issues that come their way. It's like an orchestra with every section playing not only different instruments, but different kinds of music under more than one conductor. The folly of this is obvious and maddening, but we continue to wonder why our schools experience ever-escalating problems.

We see the principal as a conductor—the leader of an orchestra that is capable of spirit-moving music played with passion and precision. The conductor can bring everyone exquisitely to the same page, playing the very same piece of music, with each part fitting together to create perfect, soul-lifting harmonies—the music made by the social curriculum as it builds inner wealth.

Any accomplished musician will tell you that, even within the restriction of playing the same piece of music as the other members of the orchestra, each musician still has great freedom. Each member of the orchestra can play in a way that is uniquely his or hers, and if it's done within the structure of the musical composition, those small variations will only enrich the final sound. Perfect. And a thousand people using the Nurtured Heart Approach are going to naturally apply it in a manner consistent with who they are. Each will have his or her very own style. Also perfect.

With an approach that's powerful and encompassing enough, the good news is that you can be far from perfect at implementing it and still derive a great deal of benefit. This is certainly not the case with so many other methods that are energetically upside-down, inadvertently rewarding negativity. The harder you push upside-down methods, the worse the situation will get.

Dennis Embry, Ph.D., is the designer of a program started in Tucson called PeaceBuilders, a community-based program that helps children learn to use nonviolent, empathic ways of communicating. Dr. Embry described an informal experiment at one school where there was much bullying, teasing, and other irksome behavior going on in the schoolyard. Schoolyard staff was doubled, but no instructions were given to this staff aside from just putting them out there as an adult presence.

The upside-down mindset continued to prevail in the schoolyard: monitors did nothing as long as things were going right and intervened when things were going wrong. The end result was that the number of problems in the schoolyard didn't decrease—they *doubled.*

More staff isn't the key. The right approach is the key. And if this sounds like the typical hard sell, keep in mind that schools can implement this approach for the price of a DVD set of presentations and perhaps a few copies of the book you now hold in your hands. There are additional costs if schools want advanced trainers to teach it and work directly with teachers (see the Resources section for information); but other schools implement the approach without spending a cent.

## Counselors Make the Perfect Experts

It is nothing short of amazing that school counselors survive their jobs as they are currently scripted. We've met many of these wonderful souls who wound up burnt to a crisp.

School counselors are expected (often, by school and district policy) to be on call at any given moment to respond to difficult children in the thick of a crisis. They are often connected to the heartbeat of the school by walkie-talkie. Counselors may be expected to enter classrooms during or just after a conflict. Their job often includes removing the offending child from the room, discussing the problems with the child, and documenting the situation for the records.

At first glance, this job description sounds well within reason and logic for a counselor. But it leaves out the fact that the same kids continue to create the same or greater levels of havoc, requiring repeated interventions. The counselor might go through her entire bag of therapeutic and disciplinary tricks and is left holding that empty bag without any significant change in the child's problems. She may not have the right tools to do so. Counselors can come to love these "problem" kids, often ending up in what feels like a positive relationship, but they can continue to fall into a few pivotal traps that are guaranteed to allow the child's world to keep spinning out of control. The situation ends up becoming totally frustrating and demoralizing for everyone involved.

Let's look at this from the point of view of the challenging child. Even if that counselor is the nicest person in the world, even if her required conversation with me about "the problem" is as good as it gets, and even if I promise that I've come to my senses and will never create the offending problem again (and think it's for real this time), I'm still experiencing in my bones the truth of the situation: *I am yet again getting more relationship as a result of my bad choices.* This will ultimately serve to deepen my impression that I get more out of life through my acts of adversity. And since most school counselors are such nice people, I'll likely "volunteer" to have that same problem and others again and again. I like the energetic hundred-dollar-bills that flow my way through the counselor. I'll continue to feel drawn to the closeness and connection of relationship with her, despite her pleas that I come to my senses.

The good news is that counselors make the some of the very best Nurtured Heart Approach experts. We've known numerous counselors who led the push for new methodology in their schools. Many have returned to their schools following a Nurtured Heart Approach seminar and asked permission to do an in-service for the staff. They follow up by meeting with teachers in small groups by grade level, where they process successes and build expertise.

Better yet, as the intervention develops, counselors find ways to re-launch their careers in a way that is more likely to yield gratification. Now they can suggest to teachers and administration that they can offer their help in a new way. Instead of pulling the child out—which usually makes the situation worse—the counselor can enter the classroom and coach the teacher to help the child in the context of the classroom while moving the entire class forward in a positive direction. This is a much better outcome for everyone involved.

We now know many counselors who have learned and embraced the Nurtured Heart Approach. They feel like they once again love their jobs. They feel deep satisfaction with having benefited the school—both teachers and children. These counselors particularly enjoy being able to call parents when things are going well, instead of the calls saying "your child has a problem" they once made so often.

## Spreading the Wealth to Parents

You probably know well that parents can end up angry, embarrassed, distressed, or even alienated when they receive calls about poor choices made by their child. If I am a parent and the child is challenging at home as well as in the classroom, I'm going to feel pretty helpless when asked to address the situation. If it's not going well at home, what on earth am I going to suggest or do that will make a difference in the classroom?

Parents are likely to be trying as hard as they can already with the methods they have at their disposal. Usually those methods involve inadvertently deepening that child's existing impression that he gets more out of life through negativity. And with normal methods, the harder a parent tries to remedy the problem, the worse the situation gets.

Here's the better alternative: Don't call the parents to report the child's problem behavior. Use the child's current negative behaviors as inspiration to heighten use of the Nurtured Heart Approach in the classroom. When the child inevitably comes around (and teachers who master this approach say it typically takes a week or two at most), then and only then call the home. This time, the call's purpose is to involve the parent in a *positive* way. By way of this call, the teacher or counselor can briefly explain the approach to share some of the magic. Here, plant the seeds for crediting the parent with some of the positive change and success.

Here's an example: Once the child—let's call him Alex—is doing well, we call his parents. We say something like, "Mrs. Jackson, I am so proud of how Alex is doing, I thought I would call to let you know. He is being wonderfully respectful and participating beautifully and intelligently in our class work. He has become one of my better students. He has responded so well to a new approach I am using with the whole class. I thought I should share just a bit of what we are doing that is working…Basically, we are making a very big deal when the children are doing anything we see that is positive. And we are being very appreciative when the kids are not breaking rules. We're refusing to give energy when any child breaks a rule. If that happens, we just provide a very quick and easy consequence—a brief time-out—and make sure that it is over quickly so we can resume the applause for successes.

"It's amazing how well it has worked with everyone, and Alex is just so wonderfully responsive that I wanted to share the good news. And I want to give you credit for all you must be doing to encourage him at home. Thanks for giving me the time to explain this. Anytime you'd like to come in and see for yourself what we're up to in the classroom, you'd be welcome."

A connection like this is so much more likely to create collaboration and camaraderie. The school staffs at Tolson and other schools around the country have seen immense benefits from this way of connecting the home and school environments. Now the parent community stands a chance of speaking the very same language as the school community; this can only help enhance inner wealth for everyone involved.

In the evening, following a tough day with his class, Mr. Y would call every student's home to report some positives to the parent or guardian. The next day he always had a stellar class. He was building positive relationship between parent and child, himself and the child, and himself and the parent.

School staff can send notes home to the parent, thanking the parent for something they are doing that is apparent in the student's character and actions. "Dear Mr. W: I gather you discuss the news with Darren. This is very helpful and important to Darren. He is proud of his world knowledge and the fact that you take time with him. You are preparing him for a great future." Notes and calls like this will reap the treasures of inner wealth.

The whole school can reach out and build the inner wealth of parents and guardians in a way that beautifully enhances the efforts of individual teachers. We are after an environment where parents can walk into school proud, even if their child is having a problem that day. Everyone has problems. We want to cultivate the ability to successfully deal with and overcome problems. We are not after more deterrents and punishments; we are after an environment so positive that it sweeps the student up into a flowing river of success. A whole-school approach makes that river so wide and so strong that everyone is swept into it! Schools can sweep parents into the current, building their inner wealth as well.

How can the school find, or even create, parental success? We know that the school has to report abuse and neglect. We know there are rules for parents to follow that the school has to enforce. We are not advocating that rules be relaxed or ignored. But we are advocating that the school pursue the positive, expect the best, and build parental inner wealth. It is very tempting to blame parents and see them as lame, bad, or hopeless; yet, if we have low expectations of parents, then they most likely will meet those expectations. Like students, parents can cover a wide spectrum from possessing abundant inner wealth to feeling they are "no good and never will be."

Just as we do with our students, we can convey to parents that they are valuable, that they belong, and that they are competent to be part of this most hopeful process. Your school might offer parent training or information about the Nurtured Heart Approach.

## The Whole-School Vision

The vision is that school is a transformative experience for students, their parents, and everyone in the school building. The school is not only producing students who perform academically, but students so ready for life that they beam optimism and confidence in themselves and their future. Maybe they are not scholars in every academic endeavor, but they are scholars at kindness, compassion, perseverance, forethought, social wisdom, friendship, and other qualities that propel great relationships and coping strategies.

Over and over, we hear principals and teachers remark that "we just can't keep doing business as usual." The current common paradigm is not working. To us, this paradigm has revolved around attempts to try and *make* students behave so that they can learn to be successful academically. It is about creating outside forces that will *make* students behave and learn. In-school suspension, detentions, calls home, sarcasm, stern lectures, and threats of alternative school are all examples of disciplinary actions common in most schools today.

The Nurtured Heart Approach is an inside-out paradigm. It is aimed directly at producing a better relationship with one's self. Common sense as well as empirical evidence tell us that change must emanate from within the student—not from external pressures based on threats or other ways of eliciting fear in the student. With the Nurtured Heart Approach, students are motivated toward improving already successful relationships, not toward stopping bad behavior to avoid punishment and shame.

If history has taught us anything, it is that punishment, shame and fear really do not work. When every person and procedure within a school is working in synchronization to validate and propel students toward a vibrant relationship with themselves and the classroom teacher, we are embracing a new paradigm—one that actually works.

The Nurtured Heart school is not set upon control and academic achievement. It is set upon the identification and creation of success for each person—the inner social curriculum. What follows from this is well-behaved students and better achievement—the external social and academic curriculums. Instead of promoting "Behave and learn so you can be a successful person," this approach tells students, "You are a successful person who can learn and behave. In fact, you ARE learning and behaving." We provide mass quantities of evidence that you already are good, valuable, and worthy and that you belong. You are more fantastic than you know.

To accomplish this, we weave the three-legged table into every aspect of the personnel and process we call school. Those three legs remain the guiding principles, whether we're dealing with four children, 40 children, 400 children, or 4,000 children. We want problems to be given as little relationship as possible, consequences to be short, and the student to be in the classroom as much as possible—preferably, students are never asked to leave the classroom because of problem behaviors. The classroom and the teacher-student relationship are where the student needs to "make it," so we want to totally convey the expectation that the student will succeed there. That is time-in!

Some people believe they need to be tough with students. They believe that students need to respect authority and that, with enough punishment, embarrassment, or messages that they are a failure, students will come to their senses and clean up their acts. The Nurtured Heart Approach promotes tremendous respect from students because they end up seeing you as an authority who is extremely generous with inner wealth, who is in control of your emotions, and who can be trusted completely. **THE REAL POWER COMES FROM THE POSITIVE SIDE OF THE EQUATION.** Rather than students coming to their senses via messages that they are bad or about to be cast out, we see students coming to their senses via evidence that they are already great and definitely belong.

Here are a few questions you might want to consider and perhaps discuss with your principal:

1. How might the Nurtured Heart Approach best fit within your district's code of conduct and your particular school?

2. How can the inner wealth of the school staff be supported and thrive?

3. How can the school involve parents and build parent/guardian inner wealth?

4. How can school staff members outside the classroom help cheer students on in success?

5. What ways can students build each other's inner wealth in class, between

classes, and before or after school?

6. What will be the role of deans, counselors, and administrators around success—and around any problems?

The Nurtured Heart Approach can be tailored to your school or district just as it can be tailored to your classroom, yet the principles of the approach should remain intact and clear in each instance.

## The Whole-School Approach in Action: When a Student Is Sent to the Office

When schools adopt this approach, they have the goal of keeping the student in the classroom. If the student has to be sent to the office, which sometimes becomes necessary despite every effort to the contrary, that student is returned to class as soon as he is "reset." Because this is an almost universal issue in schools that implement this approach, we offer some guidance on what administrators can do to maintain continuity between classroom and administrative use of the Nurtured Heart Approach.

Under this approach, the teacher would have been (1) giving the problem student time-outs or resets along with abundant reflections of success; (2) remaining very strict about the rules; and (3) not fueling the problem with negative energy (warnings, lectures, stern looks, sarcasm). If the student nevertheless has to be sent to the office, it is only because the student is violating the conduct code, or the teacher determines that too much class time will be sacrificed waiting for the student to get back to a successful time-in. We are not saying any little problem and the student is out. We are saying you have set your three-legged table solidly and given the student numerous opportunities to "reset."

As stated earlier, some students want to see if they can get the teacher to "crack" and skillfully and ingeniously pull out all the stops. Some want to get out of class to see if they can get "officially" dosed with negative energy and negative messages from administration. To them, the teacher is small potatoes compared to a megadose of relationship, albeit negative, with the most powerful people in the school.

If a teacher has done her best with the three-legged table and a student is sent to administration for further action, the administrator should make sure, first of all, to applaud the teacher for not leaking negativity, for remaining strict, and for creatively reflecting positives. It takes tremendous inner wealth on the part of the teacher to stay calm, cool, and positive in the face of an all-out challenge to spew negativity.

The second step administrators should take in this circumstance: Make sure that the school's response is to reset the student. Let the student see that you expect him to make it in the classroom. Pursue the positive, stay strict, and give no relationship or energy to the problem. Keep in mind that the ultimate success is for the student to simply have a short reset and get back into class. This paves the way for restoration of the big time-in, and he gets all the glory for doing what needed to be done to get there. He is given abundant welcome back to the class. If, however, there is a violation of code that necessitates administrative action (suspension, detention, parent conference, etc.), it needs to occur with as little fanfare as possible. Create some opportunity for the student to have a better relationship with himself (i.e., some success) that can be cheered on once the student is back in the classroom.

How can we create success for a student and a better relationship within himself even after he has been sent out of class? Creating a better relationship with one's self can be looked at as an enterprise of the body, spirit, and mind. Schools can get really creative when it comes to transforming traditional disciplinary modes into opportunities for success. For example, one school renamed in-school suspension "in-school success." While the student is out of the classroom, he is given an assignment such as writing five positive things about himself, five positive things he has done as a person that led to success in the classroom, or five things he will do to be proud of that day; those things are what the school calls home about that evening. The student may have to come up with some type of community service or act of restoration to "repair" the emotional impact of his actions. Or the student might have to list three things he could do next time to bring about a better outcome. If the incident involved aggression toward another student, he may be asked to write a report about the positive aspects of that student.

In all of this, avoid broaching "the problem," which will leak relationship to negativity.

## Ways to Support Teachers in Building Their Inner Wealth

Another essential part of the school-wide application of the approach is whole-school support for teachers. Some methods we've observed: teachers sharing success stories on a school-wide webpage; open meetings held to talk about success stories; monthly parties; visiting others' classes, where teachers cheer their colleagues on in front of students; principals popping in to surround the teacher with positive recognitions or even to give students time to praise the teacher during class. Students display tremendous sincerity when they have the opportunity to praise their teacher. We have been amazed and deeply moved by students' feelings of gratitude and appreciation for their teachers—feelings that are often completely invisible until an opportunity is given to express them. This is why we are totally convinced that YOU, the reader, are the most valuable treasure in your classroom. Students tell us so every day. YOU are a transformer of hearts, lives, and futures.

It is also essential for the administration to propel success among all school personnel and parents. How can your school recognize success in parents? How can administration propel the staff? We have a few ideas. The administration can:

- daily tour the school and praise staff
- cheer students for not getting sent to the office
- cheer students fresh from their resets
- roam the lunchroom and recognize positives
- hold success rallies for teachers and staff to share success stories
- have parent meetings to share positives
- provide a student forum for students to share success stories with their peers
- allow students to occasionally earn the privilege where they can roam classes or school and give slips of positive character recognition out to peers and teachers
- take pictures of students and teachers being successful and post them in the hall
- have parties to celebrate students as great citizens or to celebrate their acts of creative coping
- begin IEP meetings with recognition of parental success

From the minute students walk on campus to the moment they leave, they can be soaked in a sea of positives. So can teachers and other staff members. Your school needs to think about how aides can be guided to promote and reflect success in students and teachers as well as in themselves. The office and counseling staffs need to think of ways to help teachers rapidly reset when they are frustrated.

Negativity leaks and strictness are important issues for administrators, too, when the Nurtured Heart Approach is enacted school-wide. Some students love to act up just to gain pep talks with administrators. Small wonder, given what you know now.

Administrators need to eliminate as much relationship around problems as possible. One young administrator spent an inordinate amount of time sorting through the near-violent bickering of small groups of adolescent girls. Once he had them each handwrite their version of the problem for him to read later and sent them back to class without their dose of concentrated attention from him, the problems rapidly disappeared. He drained his relationship out of the problem and it vanished.

## Staff Meetings, Nurtured Heart Approach-Style

Think back to your last staff meeting. Did it start with woes and problem-solving? Most do. And staff meetings that follow on the heels of school-wide implementation of this approach are likely to start with some staff complaining about the approach or some facet of it. We have seen this situation handled adeptly by administrators and offer some guidance on how this can be accomplished.

The administrator needs to preclude any negativity about the approach by first calling on teachers who have successes that they can report and then applauding those teachers. Give this activity as much time as possible, then go on to addressing problems. But before a teacher's problems are addressed, the teacher has to talk about a few efforts he made with that student or that class that were positive uses of the approach. For example: Did the teacher refuse to energize negativity? Did he withdraw relationship from the problem and point up specific successes? This allows the principal and other teaches to applaud the teacher who has a difficult situation, giving him more positive relationship with himself in that moment. Then the group can proceed to problem-solving ideas that are consistent with the approach.

## IEP Meetings, Nurtured Heart Approach-Style

The main purpose of any IEP meeting should be to build the inner wealth of the parent. Counselors, teachers, and administrators can work together to achieve this end during IEP meetings.

A parent with a child who has hit the level of school intervention where an IEP is required probably has had years of frustration both at home and with schools. Many of these parents have lost out on a lot of joy and have received poor advice from the traditional teaching and parenting methods that don't work with challenging children. As you introduce them to the Nurtured Heart Approach, keep in mind that they are about to be immersed in a process and a language they may not understand well at all.

If parents bring an advocate to the meeting, the parents are sometimes viewed as adversarial or difficult. Let go of that view. Embrace positives. Remember that these parents live with the student in question and they have dealt with tough challenges that you may not yet recognize. These parents need help from a system that is also quite challenged. Make the IEP process about the social curriculum of the student, parent and school.

If the administration has to talk about a disciplinary action, load the meeting with both parental and student inner wealth. Have the family think as much as possible about ways to reset the student and about ways to help the student develop a better relationship with herself. Do not leak negativity, and don't invite the parent to do so either. In any exchange with parents, keep reinforcing that the rules and consequences are set by the school district. Give as little attention as possible to the consequence.

Sometimes parents feel they have to "save face" and do so by being overly critical of their own child. You can prevent the parents from entering the meeting with a negative attitude by meeting with them first to explain the type of meeting you want to have—a meeting focusing on the successes already shown by the student and the parents. Your goal is to begin building parental inner wealth. As with students, keep building and building parental inner wealth and you will ultimately see success. Chances are that the parents are already trying as hard as they can with the methods they have at their disposal. The IEP becomes an opportunity to share aspects of an approach that holds new promise.

## What to Do Next

If your school adopts Nurtured Heart, it should be consistent throughout. Create rules for the whole school in addition to those in individual classrooms so that enforcement can be strict and swift without leaking negativity. Get everyone on board, including hall monitors, bus drivers, playground monitors, and cafeteria workers. Get every staff member to a place where they're celebrating and cherishing students, but never missing a beat when a rule is broken: "Oops, broke a rule—time-out," and then getting them right back into time-in.

Choose two to three key people in your school—people who have great energy, focus, and influence—who will be the "point people" in learning the approach. They can then work with the staff of your entire school to get everyone on the same page. Principals, counselors, and master teachers are good candidates for this job

We are so impressed at the many schools that have adopted the approach on their own without spending millions of dollars on any "blue ribbon" program. Some schools that have employed the highly popular Positive Behavioral Intervention and Support (PBIS) program have "overlaid" it with the Nurtured Heart Approach with considerable success. This approach can amplify the impact of existing approaches or it can clarify what portions of existing policy need to be altered or abandoned.

# Two Principals Share Their Thoughts

## Maria Figueroa, M.Ed.

*Principal, Tolson Elementary School, Tucson, Arizona*

Back in 2000, when I was appointed to Tolson Elementary School, no school-wide discipline policy or program was in place. Dealing with student discipline took up 75 percent of my workday. Students were not respecting each other on the playground or in the classrooms. Once the lunch recesses began at 10:30 a.m., there was a constant line of at least 15 students waiting their turn to meet the principal to receive their sentences (consequences) for hitting, cursing, racial slurring, or other infractions. Students were sent to my office for discipline without written referrals from lunch monitors and classroom teachers.

Many students and teachers expected the principal to physically remove students from the classroom when they refused to comply with teachers' orders to go to the office. Students were accustomed to getting attention while being embarrassed in front of their peers and removed from their classrooms. Misbehavior was allowed to continue until it became extremely disruptive to both teachers and students.

With some available funds, I formed a discipline committee to come up with a school-wide discipline program. One of the teachers on that committee had heard of the Nurtured Heart Approach. Following some research, I found four programs that dealt with the issues we were facing at Tolson; the Nurtured Heart Approach was one of them. I purchased a copy of the book *Transforming the Difficult Child: The Nurtured Heart Approach,* along with three other books and articles.

Howard Glasser and Jenn Easley's book was the only how-to book that really had a blueprint for teachers and parents on how to deal with difficult children in a respectful manner. This approach addressed the lack of respect and the issues of due process we were experiencing at our school. The discipline committee ended up selecting the Nurtured Heart Approach as the guide and format for our school's discipline plan.

It was through serendipity and research that I found out the designer of this approach, Howard Glasser, worked and lived in Tucson. After the school staff read the book, I invited Howard to speak to teachers and parents at Tolson. (He has been a guest speaker at Tolson on several occasions, and we purchase his book to give to our new teachers and parents.)

While the committee did their homework and held meetings on all four proposed discipline programs, I began to implement the Nurtured Heart Approach at home with my three-year-old son. He was a prime candidate for the ADHD label. He was all over the place in his school, and all the adults had problems controlling his behavior. I was even told by a teacher's assistant in his school that I should take him to the doctor because he might be autistic. At work, I constantly reminded teachers not to encourage parents to take their children to the doctor when they were having behavior issues. Now, as the tables turned and my child was the one being given a diagnosis by a teacher, I felt even more committed to a shift both at work and at home.

I had success at home using the Nurtured Heart Approach with my son and was pleased when the school's discipline committee selected this approach. A few other teachers in our school also had success using the Nurtured Heart Approach at home with their children. One year after the approach had been used consistently by all the adults at Tolson, I decided to enroll my own son in this school. Almost every teacher on staff has done the same with their children and grandchildren.

At Tolson, the teachers and I worked together to create a discipline plan and procedures that mirror the Nurtured Heart Approach philosophy. Howard assisted us in wording our school rules and creating consequences that would show students exactly what is expected of them. Adults and students alike expect discipline with due process, consistency, respect, and no chances but consequences. When substitute teachers break one of the Nurtured Heart rules, students let us know.

Each year the entire Tolson staff reads or re-reads the book *Transforming the Difficult Child*. We have channeled all our energy into giving attention to students when they are behaving in appropriate, acceptable ways. We also created "praise notes" that all adults give to students to recognize them for their hard work, effort and acceptable behaviors.

I find that when the Nurtured Heart Approach is implemented in a building, adults begin to show respect for students *and* their adult colleagues. The approach has made Tolson a wonderful place to work; our teacher attrition rate stabilized to less than one percent for four years in a row.

Several students at Tolson had been labeled ADHD and some were on medication when we first began to work with the Nurtured Heart Approach in our classrooms. A couple of those students were taken off their meds once teachers at Tolson began to work with them in classrooms. We have had several families bring their children to Tolson as an alternative to placing the child on ADHD medications. Here, teachers are more likely to refer challenging students to GATE (Gifted and Talented Education) programs than to special education programs. Currently, in Tolson's student population of 515 students, only seven students are receiving special education services; 58 students are enrolled in GATE classes.

The biggest challenge for us has been to keep giving praise notes and constant praise to students and resisting the urge to give attention to negative behaviors. After about four years of using the approach, adults seem to turn a corner and master this, and they automatically accentuate the positive. We make an effort to work with new employees and substitutes new to the school, helping them meld with the whole-school use of this approach. Here's my advice to educators embarking on this journey: *Be consistent* with constant praise and consequences. The length of the consequence does not matter; it is the consistency that is important. Respect children while implementing the strategies. *Be patient.* In some cases it takes a long time to elicit the encouraged behaviors. Keep in mind that, up to this point, the student's inappropriate behaviors are what have been noticed by most adults, and they need time to see and trust that things are going to be different from now on.

## Susan Zola, Ph.D.
*Principal, Jefferson Middle School, Champaign, Illinois.*

Over the past 22 years, I have searched for a model that honors the best in our youth. The Nurtured Heart Approach does that and much more.

In the spring of 2006, upon reviewing our school's discipline data, I noted a common trend: a small core group of students was involved in a majority of the school incidents. A staff member had heard of the Nurtured Heart Approach and asked me to hear a brief presentation from representatives. The model was based on solid logic that humans respond to whatever evidence is offered to them over the course of time. If youths hear they are attentive, studious, forward-thinking, good planners, and in possession of other positive character traits, that is what they will embrace. If they are bombarded only with rules, they will establish a strong guard and hesitancy within the school culture.

The Nurtured Heart school promotes high levels of evidence that students are successful from the moment they walk through the door. "You're late" is replaced with "Welcome, and we are pleased you are here today." Teachers, administrators and support staff work to resist the temptation to lecture. Instead, they offer overwhelming evidence that students are on track for success.

When a student has a lapse in judgment, consequences are provided in a consistent manner. Students learn that we all have problems and that they are much more than their problems. Within the classroom setting, resets are commonly used to get students back on track: a moment to regroup, refocus and reclaim success for the day.

Nurtured Heart schools have clear, consistent expectations enforced by all, for all. Arriving to class on time is the expectation. Moving respectfully through the hallway becomes commonplace. Bringing your materials to class, ready for success, becomes the norm. The work of adults within the setting begins to shift. Their energy and time are focused on building young hearts and minds. When students are unfocused, teachers offer time to regroup—given without energy or emotion—and then welcome them back.

Our work at building a Nurtured Heart school is early in its development. The feedback from those who have adopted the approach is quite encouraging. Time will determine its impact on the youth assigned to our care and on the adults. Do we, as educators, have the power to transform lives and build up the capacity of our youth? I firmly believe we do.

# Conclusion

## *Inside Out*

WE KNOW MANY CHILDREN PERSONALLY who quietly live in a realm of inner glory. It's not about accruing external markings of success for their own sake; they possess an inner destination of experiencing life's joy and potential for exploration. The landmarks of success are definitely desired and appreciated, but the prevailing focus is one of being in touch with his or her life force and finding ways of flourishing that are in keeping with his or her true self.

Howie Glasser's own 15-year-old daughter comes to mind. He is in awe of how in touch with her feelings she is; how kind and considerate to others; how she always seems to want to do the right things for her own unique reasons; how she loves to express her life force creatively. Also inspiring is the depth to which she enjoys her friends, her tasks and her life in such an unassuming manner—this enjoyment is as natural to her and as easy for her as breathing. She figures so many things out for herself because her inner wealth seems to work not only as a compass but as a propelling, compelling, intelligent force. She never has to be told to get good grades or to get her work done or do it well. She wants to do all this and more, of her own volition. She doesn't seem to have a need to have problems or to carry negative thoughts. If she has a trying situation or a rough edge, she just experiences it and gets past it so quickly. Her default setting seems to be set simply to *being*.

The Nurtured Heart Approach strives to intentionally create the characteristics we find so compelling in young people like Howie's daughter. Left in the hands of such balanced, compassionate young people—and there are lots and lots of kids like her out there coming of age—the world is bound to change in wonderful ways!

This approach works by affecting children's core sense of being. The child then winds up radiating this out to the world. By working with students in this way, we help make the world a more peaceful place.

Any change that matters and lasts will come from the inside out. No one can be forced into an act of courage. They say they found the courage to act. Where did they find it? Inside. No one says they were forced into loving another. Where does this feeling occur? Inside. Why did you become a teacher? Was it external constraints, rules, threats or punishments? Very likely, it was something inside.

It is the inside stuff that helps you tolerate, overcome, connect, and succeed at what you do. It is what brought you to this point in this book. You have a hope, a dream, and the ability to challenge yourself to achieve it. You would not have picked this book up without those qualities inside.

Your self-esteem may have been marred by numerous outside forces, yet you continue to seek a better way. That is your inner wealth sustaining and propelling you forward toward greater relationships—especially with your dreams and hopes. What do you really suppose are the hopes and dreams of your students and the adults raising them? Give your dreams and hopes, and theirs, real life. Find the evidence that you and they have the abilities and qualities to continue on the quest. Find so much evidence, create so much inner wealth, that you and they can fearlessly pursue a positive future. The force *is* with you. Inside.

# A Recap:

## *The Nurtured Heart Approach Basics*

## Purpose

The Nurtured Heart Approach is a social curriculum that transforms students' character and spirit, giving them a deep conviction that they can cope with problems and succeed socially and emotionally. We refer to this personal power as inner wealth.

## Basic Perspectives

- **Difficult children are seeking intense relationship.**
- Difficult kids quickly learn that they can readily engage and control others through negative behavior. These children can become almost addicted to the rush of this kind of relationship.
- Ordinary parenting and classroom discipline methods make things worse with children like this, because most normal methods demonstrate more relationship and energy when things are going wrong—and, in contrast, little energy and relationship when things are going well.
- Children who possess sufficient inner wealth do not need negative relationships, because they can sustain themselves by connecting to the world and to themselves through successes. The more inner wealth, the greater the resiliency.
- There is no way to avoid teaching a social curriculum. We are always sending some message.

## Basic Principles

- Create a rich relationship by creatively energizing success. We call this "time-in."
- Create an empty, boring "time-out" that consists of the child missing out on life's energies and relationships. The child is out of the loop; you are refusing to give energy and relationship to negativity. Instead, you are giving an unceremonious consequence.
- Have a clear line between time-in and time-out.

- Always work toward a positive future time-in.

- Always let students be fully responsible for their problems. Don't deny them the result of a poor choice—a consequence—when a rule is broken.

- Always treat them as though they are fully competent, *right now.*

- When interacting with students, control your mood and the direction of conversations. Do not leak negativity by giving energy and relationship to poor behaviors.

- There is nothing we can do to stop bad behavior, but we can consequence or celebrate whatever behavior does occur. We have exquisite control when we are strict (consequence for any rule broken) and positive (create and celebrate successes with acknowledgment and recognition) and when we avoid leaking negativity.

- How to accomplish transformation: the three-legged table

  - **Pursue the Positive:** Find example after example of moments where students are coping well, making good decisions, regaining self-control, and showing great character. Recognize these positives and reflect them back to students, giving them an ever-growing body of evidence that they are valuable, competent, and belong in a positive life. Hold up the mirror!

  - **No Negativity Leaks:** By not giving problems and poor choices a lot of your relationship time, attention, and energy, you teach students their problems do not defeat or upset you and that they do not have to have problems in order to achieve relationship with adults. At the same time, you are proving to them that their positive behavior will lead to relationship success. Problems become unnecessary as a way to gain relationship.

  - **Strictness:** There is no need for reminders, lectures, investigations, or exceptions. The rules are the rules and are enforced consistently, constantly, calmly and strictly. The "game" is easy to learn and succeed at because the rules are clear.

- The consequence is a time-out that is kept short as a way to purposefully lead to further successes.

- Always be in the truth of the moment, like the lens of a camera. After the time-out is over and the problem is no longer happening, create new ways to applaud the child's current choices as demonstrations of success.

- Acknowledge that staying positive yourself and "modeling the model" is hard work sometimes. When you fall off the horse, forgive yourself, remind yourself of what you're here to do, and get back on.

## Potential Problems and Solutions

- Get great at finding "gold in the septic tank." Sometimes it's hard to see the good. Creating successes is an art, and anyone can learn to do this with the techniques offered in this book.

- Don't back off on praise when things go well. When your classroom turns around, continue to *pour it on!*

- Compliments like "good job" and "thank you" are too under-energized and too vague to transform your students. Children need more detailed, elaborate, artful feedback to point out their attributes of greatness and feed their inner wealth. You cannot be too positive.

- Remember: if a student is extremely disruptive and you keep the three-legged table standing strong, you have succeeded! The student's poor choice remains his problem, not yours. Invest no energy, relationship or emotion into those problems. Instead, show him that you have total trust in his ability to solve them himself. Create evidence to support his belief in your trust by applauding the absence of the problem once the consequence has ended. Let him know how great a choice he's making right now.

# Resources

## Web site

There is a web site that supports the use of the Nurtured Heart Approach and the work of the Children's Success Foundation. That web site is:

**www.difficultchild.com**

Two features in particular are noteworthy. One is a listing by state of all those who have received Advanced NHA Training and who have become certified trainers. Contact information is contained on the "coaching" page, and many of these trainers are available for consultations and presentations. Second is an online discussion forum where anyone can pose an issue, a question or a success and in most instances receive one or more responses from those who visit the forum on a regular basis—almost like an online support group.

## Books

The two books below are available for purchase at amazon.com and through the web site listed above.

*Transforming the Difficult Child: The Nurtured Heart Approach* by Howard Glasser, MA, and Jennifer Easley, MA (1998)

*101 Reasons to Avoid Ritalin Like the Plague (Including One Great Reason Why It's Almost Always Unnecessary)* by Howard Glasser, MA (2005)